Kerala, 1956 to the Present

'Kerala is different, but not in the way we think.' Economic change in this southern state of India has fascinated economists. Most studies have focused on the state's unusual human development, and asked how a poor and economically stagnant state could achieve high levels of education and healthcare. These works point to politics and government policy to answer the question. History, this book says, shows that the foundations of human development were laid before the formation of the state and were owed to many factors besides politics. The striking point about the state in recent decades is not human development but income growth, which has been faster than most states since the 1990s. The question this book asks is: how could an income-poor state break out of stagnation so dramatically? The answers consider past globalisation, labour mobility, a legacy of welfare spending, and the positive ways these features interacted since India's economic reforms.

Tirthankar Roy is Professor of Economic History at the London School of Economics and Political Science. He has taught and published extensively on South Asian history and development. His most recent monographs include *A Business History of India: Enterprise and the Emergence of Capitalism from 1700* (Cambridge University Press, 2018) and *The Reserve Bank of India Vol. 5, 1997–2008* (Cambridge University Press, 2022).

K. Ravi Raman is a member of the State Planning Board in the Government of Kerala. He is the author of *Global Capital and Peripheral Labour* (Routledge, 2010). His next monograph, *Political Ecospatiality: Livelihood, Environment, and Subaltern Struggles in Kerala*, is forthcoming from Cambridge University Press.

ECONOMIC HISTORY OF INDIAN STATES

The economic history of India has two strands – the story of the Union as a whole and the singular narratives of the individual states – both of which are equally important. While studies have focused on the Indian economy as a single entity, the books in this series take a more granular view of its history.

This series consists of short coursebooks that integrate history, politics, and development into single, state-specific accounts of regional economic histories that are an intrinsic part of the nation's larger economic account. Rather than presenting an argument, they synthesize existing material into an accessible story about how the economies of the states have changed in the last seven decades.

While the national and international context will be discussed wherever relevant, the volumes primarily seek to clarify the distinctive features of a state's economic history and convey its unique historical narrative.

Editorial Board

Tirthankar Roy is Professor of Economic History at the London School of Economics and Political Science.

Abhirup Sarkar is Retired Professor of Economics at the Indian Statistical Institute, Kolkata.

Anand Swamy is Professor of Economics at Williams College, Williamstown, MA.

Kerala, 1956 to the Present

India's Miracle State

Tirthankar Roy
K. Ravi Raman

CAMBRIDGE
UNIVERSITY PRESS

Shaftesbury Road, Cambridge CB2 8EA, United Kingdom

One Liberty Plaza, 20th Floor, New York, NY 10006, USA

477 Williamstown Road, Port Melbourne, VIC 3207, Australia

314–321, 3rd Floor, Plot 3, Splendor Forum, Jasola District Centre, New Delhi – 110025, India

103 Penang Road, #05–06/07, Visioncrest Commercial, Singapore 238467

Cambridge University Press is part of Cambridge University Press & Assessment, a department of the University of Cambridge.

We share the University's mission to contribute to society through the pursuit of education, learning and research at the highest international levels of excellence.

www.cambridge.org
Information on this title: www.cambridge.org/9781009521635

© Tirthankar Roy and K. Ravi Raman 2024

First published 2024

A catalogue record for this publication is available from the British Library

ISBN 978-1-009-52163-5 Hardback
ISBN 978-1-009-52165-9 Paperback

Contents

List of Tables and Figures   vii
Preface   ix

1 Introduction   1
2 Before Independence   16
3 The Retreat of Agriculture   41
4 Capital: Retreat and Resurgence   56
5 Work, Labour and Migration   82
6 Growth and Development   99
7 The Left Legacy   119
8 Geography: An Asset or a Challenge?   134
9 Conclusion   144

References   150
Index   163

Tables and Figures

Tables

6.1 Literacy rate (%)   101

6.2 Population 1901–2011 (million)   107

6.3 Sector shares in domestic product (%)   110

Figures

1.1 Kerala as a proportion of India (%)   5

6.1 Population, Kerala (right axis) and India in millions   107

6.2 Per capita income (constant prices) of Kerala as a percentage of all-India, 1980–2013   110

Preface

The series to which this book belongs began with the intuition that the pathway of economic change since independence from colonial rule (1947) differed fundamentally between the states of India because their prehistory, geography, political make-up and initial conditions were very different. So large is the difference that each case deserves a book. Contributions to the series will inevitably structure their work to adapt to the specific experience of the states and cannot follow a single template. In that decision, one thing matters: whether to write a chronological narrative or a thematic one.

There is no ideal choice. We decided to follow the thematic format because we wished to concentrate on the main drivers of economic change, like migration, trends in private investment or environmental change, which did not unfold in a coordinated way. We felt a chronological story suggesting that the 1970s saw one kind of change and the 1980s another would miss the point. Still, to keep chronology in the foreground, we discuss the changing character of the state's economy in the introduction and the conclusion (Chapters 1 and 9).

We wish to acknowledge the anonymous readers of the book proposal, and the reader of the manuscript, for their comments and suggestions that significantly improved the quality of this text. We thank Upasana Guha, who provided valuable research assistance, for her careful and diligent work. The help rendered by Rachel Mathew, Dulhaqe S. and Benna Fathima is also gratefully acknowledged.

A note on placenames: Many placenames have changed since 1956. In every chapter, in the first usage we write both old and new names and use the changed name in the rest of the chapter. Chapter 2 on history uses the old names in subsequent usages.

T.R.

K.R.R.

1

Introduction

The Miracle

In 1981, the south Indian state of Kerala was among the poorest regions in India. The state's average income was about a third smaller than the national average. In the late 1970s, by average income, Kerala was in the bottom third of India's thirty-odd states. In 2022, per capita income in the state was 50–60 per cent higher than the national average.[1] Among those states large in land size, populous and with a diversified economic base, the state was the fifth richest in terms of average income in 2022. Gujarat, Karnataka, Tamil Nadu and Telangana were the other four. None of the others saw such a sharp change in relative ranking.

Kerala's economy did not grow steadily throughout these forty years. The acceleration, catching up and overtaking were not more than fifteen years old, twenty at the most. Income growth rates were low for much of the 1980s and the 1990s. The numbers changed sharply only in recent decades. The roots of this extraordinary growth performance, however, were much older. This book is a search for these roots.

It is not a common practice among economists to treat a state in India as the subject of long-term economic history. But 'Kerala is different' from all other Indian states.[2] A huge scholarship building from the 1970s and drawing in many social scientists insisted it was different. Although poor, the population

---

[1] In 1960, the state had a per capita income of 265 rupees; the Indian average was 306 rupees. Until 1980, the divergence held steady. After that, there was a catchup. In 2021–23, the average income of the state stood at 148,790 rupees, while the average for India was 98,374 rupees.

[2] Polly Hill, 'Kerala Is Different', *Modern Asian Studies* 20, no. 4 (1986): 779–92.

of the state lived much longer than the average Indian and had a significantly higher literacy rate than in the rest of India. The scholarship trying to explain this anomaly was mindful of history. But the history had a narrow purpose. It was made to work for a specific question: how did an income-poor region make great strides in human development? The discourse that emerged to answer the question had two critical weaknesses. First, it was too state-focused and neglected to analyse enough market-led changes. Second, it took income poverty for granted. Neither the question nor the answers offered are useful to explain the recent acceleration in income. The explanations could not show how the basic premise of a low income might change someday because the research agenda did not consider that prospect very likely.

Our book attempts to explain the long-term pattern of economic change by studying economic history. The income trend figures centrally. The interpretation considers four main factors in their mutual interaction: a tradition of engagement with the world economy that dates back centuries; a rich reserve of commercially exploitable natural resources; an abundance of literate workers; and an activist leftist political tradition that started as a movement against inequality but morphed into regimes that pursued growth with help from the private capitalist sector. These factors did not work in concert. For decades after the formation of the state in 1956, the political tradition suppressed some forms of transactions between Kerala and the world economy. But that changed in the 1990s, and the four factors started to align in a mutually compatible manner. As they did, Kerala rediscovered the comparative advantage it had lost in the 1970s.

Because this state (unlike most other Indian states) has been the subject of a large discourse in applied development studies, it is fair to start with a reference to that scholarship.

'Kerala Is Different'

A large and 'to some extent [*sic*] learned' scholarship, said the social anthropologist Polly Hill, claimed that Kerala was unlike 'the great agricultural plains areas [of India], which for centuries before the British had experienced large-scale political organisation' (the historian Eric Stokes, cited by Hill). Its coastal position, semi-equatorial climate, maritime tradition, mixed-faith society and princely rule in one part set it apart. Hill, like Stokes, did not say how that mattered. Most general interpretations of the region's economic history went, like this one, in a speculative and incomplete manner and 'to some extent learned'.

When Hill wrote this piece, Kerala had progressed from being just different to being a model. About ten years earlier, a landmark study, *Poverty, Unemployment and Development Policy: A Case Study with Reference to Kerala*, published by the United Nations, had projected the state as the case that showed the possibility of attaining high levels of human development at a relatively low level of income.[3] In the 1980s, the concept of development embraced human development, and Kerala offered a message of hope among economies otherwise trapped in low income and weak growth.

The state became a model precisely because it was income-poor and had low income growth. Measured in average income, 'Kerala is overwhelmingly poor,' wrote Richard Franke and Barbara Chasin in 1992 in the *Earth Island Journal*. 'If it were an independent country, it would be the ninth poorest in the world.'[4] And yet, it had 'the world's highest levels of health care, education and social justice to the area', a unique profile in the developing world and India. In 1981, the literacy rate was above 70 per cent, against 40 for India. In 1981, the literacy rate for females in the state was 65 per cent (a little lower than for males), 40 per cent higher than male literacy for India, and 160 per cent higher than female literacy. All over India, cities had a distinctly better developmental profile than villages. In this state, the inequality disappeared. For example, urban and rural literacy rates were nearly equal. Infant mortality rates showed a similar difference from the Indian pattern.

According to Franke and Chasin, Kerala showed how development could happen even in a poor society. It challenged the right-leaning academic obsessed with growth rates in the gross domestic product (GDP), who said that nations needed income growth first, the benefits of which would spread through society via tax-funded public expenditure and private expenditure on healthcare and education. Instead, income growth was not needed at all for education and healthcare. A sound redistribution system of limited gains was all that was required.

For the left-leaning academic, the message was that radical redistributive policies worked wonders. Kerala, Prabhat Patnaik said in the *Social Scientist*

---

[3] United Nations, *Poverty, Unemployment and Development Policy: A Case Study of Selected Issues with Reference to Kerala* (New York: United Nations, 1975).

[4] Richard Franke and Barbara Chasin, 'Kerala: Development Without Growth', *Earth Island Journal* 7, no. 2 (1992): 25–26.

in 1995, besides gaining from a 'long history of struggles unleashed by the powerful Communist movement', also had a different economic structure. It had 'an internally-balanced production-structure where it is self-sufficient in basic necessities'. For the rest of the Global South, the lesson was that socialistic self-reliance was desirable, and capitalistic globalisation was unnecessary, even undesirable. 'All those who look upon the Kerala trajectory as a worthwhile model for the third world … cannot but oppose the implementation of Fund-Bank-dictated economic "reforms" ,' Patnaik concluded.[5] There was something right in this emphasis on politics and distribution. One of the most unequal societies even by Indian standards before 1947, the region's brutal caste hierarchy had come under attack by a range of political and social forces including the communists.

Still, by 1990, the model and its message of hope were fast losing their lustre. No one disputed that Kerala was different, but the euphoria over that statement was dying. Experts based in the state were the first to attack it. It was unsustainable in a regime of low economic growth and consequent strains on the state finances, said K. K. George in 1999.[6] In 2003, P. D. Jeromi reiterated the message with more force.[7] In 2000, K. T. Rammohan said that the Kerala Model had hollowed out conceptually.[8] By hiding many social ills, the concept did not persuade, carried too many preconceptions and did not represent anything virtuous anymore. By then, money coming in from outside the state had changed its economy unrecognisably. Well into that process, K. Ravi Raman wrote that growing dependence on foreign borrowing in the state could put pressure on the sustainability of the Kerala Model.[9]

[5] Prabhat Patnaik, 'The International Context and the "Kerala Model"', *Social Scientist* 23, nos. 1/3 (1995): 37–49.
[6] K. K. George, *Limits to Kerala Model of Development: An Analysis of Fiscal Crisis and Its Implications* (Trivandrum: Centre for Development Studies, 1993).
[7] P. D. Jeromi, 'What Ails Kerala's Economy: A Sectoral Exploration', *Economic and Political Weekly* 38, no. 16 (2003): 1584–600.
[8] K. T. Rammohan, 'Assessing Reassessment of Kerala Model', *Economic and Political Weekly* 35, no. 15 (2000): 1234–36.
[9] K. Ravi Raman, 'Asian Development Bank, Policy Conditionalities and the Social Democratic Governance: Kerala Model under Pressure?' *Review of International Political Economy* 16, no. 2 (2009): 284–308. See also essays in K. Ravi Raman (ed.), *Development, Democracy and the State: Critiquing Kerala Model of Development* (London and New York: Routledge, 2010).

These scepticisms are significant but limited tools to explain the long-term trajectory of change. We do not dispute that the state did have unusual levels of achievements in human development. But this is not the story we find either interesting or worthy of a serious explanation. This book addresses a different puzzle altogether.

The Task before Us

The task before us can be described with reference to Figure 1.1. The chart has three lines; two of these lines measure social development, specifically literacy and life expectancy. The third measures economic growth (per capita income). In all cases, the lines trace the state's position relative to India.

The social development proxies show a higher level than India throughout but a long-term convergence between Kerala and India. The state had a better record than India, but only initially. Since independence, both the state and India have improved life expectancy and literacy. Indeed, what the state did, India did even faster. The India model was not fundamentally different from the Kerala Model, and was possibly more interesting than the latter.

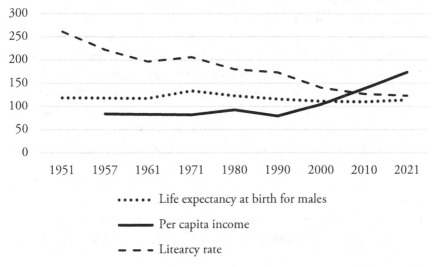

Figure 1.1   Kerala as a proportion of India (%)

Source: The sources are various documents available in the public domain, but principally the Indian censuses and State Planning Board datasets.

All that remains to be explained is the *initial difference in levels*. Demographers have a simple explanation for the level of difference in life expectancy – benign semi-equatorial climatic conditions in the state, compared with the semi-arid tropical conditions in much of southern and western India with a history of droughts, famines, periodic food and water shortages, and epidemic disease. 'It is quite possible that Kerala held this advantage [in mortality] for a long period in history,' two authorities on population history write, 'due to favourable climatological conditions and scattered pattern of settlement that might have helped in arresting the spread of epidemics….'[10] The more modest change in life expectancy line in Figure 1.1 represents the persistence of a geographical advantage.

The initial advance in education is a little more complicated. The two default stories in popular history discourses are that this was a gift from enlightened princely rulers, whereas British colonial rulers neglected public goods in much of South Asia, and that the communists delivered or forced states to deliver more welfare spending. Both are crude and uninformed narratives. Modern Kerala contained both colonial and independent territories. British-ruled Malabar did fall behind the southern region, but then the southern region had greater taxable capacity than British India thanks to a different economic structure (Chapter 6). Princely states did not spend much money on defence because British India subsidised their defence. There were non-state agents behind the education drive: the Christian church, a powerful social reform movement as a counter to brutal forms of inequality that the princes did little to redress, and competition between communities. From before the Travancore rulers took up the cause of mass education, the Christian missions pursued that cause. Specific patterns of market exchange must be factored in. Kerala exported people to service-sector jobs inside India and abroad on a large scale and much before other states in India began to do it. That history of labour export might account for a part of the incentive to acquire education.

No matter the explanation for the head-start, the post-independence trend in social development is too unsurprising and uninteresting to write a book about. All that the trend says is that the state held its commitment to spend on schools and hospitals, whereas the rest of India quickly caught up in

---

[10] P. N. Mari Bhat and S. Irudaya Rajan, 'Demographic Transition in Kerala Revisited', *Economic and Political Weekly* 25, nos. 35–26 (1990): 1957–80.

the same endeavour. The truly interesting story about Kerala is not its social development, but the shift in relative economic growth from a falling-behind in the 1980s to a forging-ahead (the income line in Figure 1.1). That needs explaining because there is clearly a structural shift here. Education and life expectancy do not explain that in any obvious way.

Two decades into the new millennium, the state was one of the vanguards in the country's post-liberalisation growth resurgence. From the mid-1990s, economic liberalisation (implementing a part of the so-called Fund–Bank recipe) was underway in India. Kerala joined the neo-liberal bandwagon. By 2022, it represented another anomaly – a Marxist state presiding over a robust capitalist resurgence. Its income growth has been consistently and significantly above the national average since 2000. With population growth approaching near-zero, GDP growth translated into a relatively higher per capita income growth compared with the north Indian states. Far from being 'overwhelmingly poor', as Franke and Chasin called it twenty-five years earlier, Kerala had an average income between 50 and 80 per cent higher than the Indian average in the 2010s and comparable to most middle-income countries. In this respect, it was not unique anymore. It was part of a growth resurgence in greater south India, including Tamil Nadu, Karnataka and Telangana, if not Andhra Pradesh. All four states registered GDP growth rates double or more than the Indian average in the 2010s.

How credibly have scholars explained the growth resurgence?

An Unexplained Puzzle

One strand in the scholarship on the state's trajectory, which had once made heavy intellectual investment in the Kerala Model, almost overlooks the growth resurgence. Jean Drèze and Amartya Sen, whose writings have had a deep impact on the debate, acknowledge the turnaround and explain it with reference to social development: '[T]he improvement of living conditions in the state has not only continued but even accelerated, with help from rapid economic growth, which in turn has been assisted by the state's focus on elementary education and other basic capabilities.'[11] Other experts repeat

---

[11] Jean Drèze and Amartya Sen, *An Uncertain Glory: India and Its Contradictions* (Princeton: Princeton University Press, 2013), 70.

this sentiment: 'High public spending on social sectors ... provides a positive thrust to economic growth.'[12]

This is not credible. This is not what Figure 1.1 tells us. These bland claims do not say how easier access to primary schools and longer lives translate into economic growth. There is no obvious connection between the cause and the effect because economic growth stems from skilling and investment, not the ability to read and write. The claims say nothing about the huge shifts in patterns of market participation that lie behind skilling and revival of private investment. Nor does it answer why, if there was a direct relationship between basic capability and economic growth, Kerala fell behind in economic growth in the 1980s after fifty years of staying ahead in social development. Why did it not experience a growth resurgence much earlier? And, if India did relatively better than Kerala in social development, why did India not register even higher income growth?

Other scholars more focused on specific themes rather than the deep roots of development have discussed these trends, with partial success. The emergence of interstate inequality since the economic reforms of the 1990s has preoccupied Indian economists for some time. Many studies measured convergence and divergence among Indian states and discussed what the results tell us about sources of economic growth in general.[13] These investigations miss the trees for the wood. The reader drowns in details of measurement procedures to notice the distinct patterns of change in the states. Any general claim about reasons for statistical convergence or divergence requires a sense of how comparable the states are. That issue is hardly discussed.

Of the region-bound scholarships, one strand offers many lessons relevant to the present project, one that studies international migration and demographic change. This strand took off in the late 1980s mainly to document and explain the migration of large numbers of Malayali people to

---

[12] Jayan Jose Thomas, 'The Achievements and Challenges of the Kerala "Model"', *India Forum*, https://www.theindiaforum.in/article/achievements-challenges-kerala-model (accessed 1 February 2024).

[13] For a selection of these studies, see Dipankar Dasgupta, Pradip Maiti, Robin Mukherjee, Subrata Sarkar and Subhendu Chakrabarti, 'Growth and Interstate Disparities in India', *Economic and Political Weekly* 35, no. 27 (2000): 2413–22; Amaresh Dubey, 'Intra-State Disparities in Gujarat, Haryana, Kerala, Orissa and Punjab', *Economic and Political Weekly* 44, nos. 26/27 (2009): 224–30.

the Persian Gulf states. Over the next three decades, the literature matured, taking on more ambitious tasks like assessing the impact of mass migration for work on regional and urban economies and families and exploring the interconnection between human development, demographic shifts, gender inequality and international migration. These are ingredients in our story. Nevertheless, seen as an economic history, the scholarship is insufficient. It does not say much about the growth resurgence, its prehistory and its origin.

A cluster of writings published in the last twenty years addressed the growth turnaround, if tentatively. A first attempt to reread the recent times happened in a 2005 symposium on Kerala in the *Economic and Political Weekly*. P. D. Jeromi said that a state notoriously unfriendly to private investors became more friendly in the early 2000s. The earlier sentiment was, according to this analysis, a reaction to the exploitative nature of foreign capitalists in the region in the princely state days.[14] There is no evidence that the average Malayali thought badly of plantation owners or commodity traders from Britain. Certainly, the princes did not think that way. If capital as such was evil, why did the sentiment change?

K. P. Kannan's reading of a possible turnaround was more substantial but not too dissimilar.[15] A statistical study of growth and inequality published in 2016 observed that there was a growth acceleration with rising inequality, and that both tendencies were 'new'. However, to drive that point, it is necessary to engage fully with history, that is, to show what this was a change from, which was beyond the scope of the paper.[16] In perhaps the most comprehensive overview of the turnaround so far, a recent article by Kannan suggests that the remittances consolidated investment in human capital, and that the turnaround did owe to a reintegration of the region's economy with the world economy.[17] We agree and use this thesis in the book. Kannan's reference point, however, was not the state's own long-term historical trajectory, but the Kerala Model of development.

[14] P. D. Jeromi, 'Economic Reforms in Kerala', *Economic and Political Weekly* 40, no. 30 (2005): 3267–77.

[15] K. P. Kannan, 'Kerala's Turnaround in Growth: Role of Social Development, Remittances and Reform', *Economic and Political Weekly* 40, no. 6 (2005): 548–54.

[16] A. P. Sreeraj and Vamsi Vakulabharanam, 'High Growth and Rising Inequality in Kerala since the 1980s', *Oxford Development Studies* 44, no. 4 (2016): 367–83.

[17] K. P. Kannan, 'Kerala "Model" of Development Revisited: A Sixty-Year Assessment of Successes and Failures', *Indian Economic Journal* 71, no. 1 (2023): 120–51.

That leaves us with a rich and insufficiently explored question. Can we have one story that can explain both the long stagnation and the recent acceleration in GDP growth? In this book, we do that by stressing four big agents of change: a history of globalisation, resource endowments, distinct demographics and distinct politics.

Globalisation and Resource Endowments

This region of India had forged deep connections with West Asia, Europe and the rest of India through trade, migration and foreign investment centuries before the modern era. A long coastline with relatively easy access to the Arabian Sea ports and, via these, to Europe was one of the geographical advantages. Many seaboard areas in India developed a commercial heritage. Something else marked this region as an attractive trading zone.

Whereas most of India is monsoon tropical, that is, has a long dry and often extremely hot summer and a short and intense rainy period due to the actions of the monsoons, Kerala has a more temperate semi-equatorial climate. Tropical heat and aridity are missing, or weak, in most parts of it. The southwest monsoon makes landfall on these coasts bringing in exceptionally heavy rain. Combined with a mountainous geography along its eastern borders, the monsoon and moderate summers make for a unique natural resource situation. With far more water per head than the rest of India, rice is grown almost everywhere. Indeed, until the early twentieth century, the region exported some rice. Although agricultural land is not abundant, the region has long been relatively free from famines and droughts.

Foreign merchants who came to trade on these coasts valued the cheap subsistence and the low cost of food and water. The climate, soil and the vast patches of saltwater marshes sustained natural coconut groves. The extensive forests in the east were a source of herbs and spices. In the nineteenth century, forests were cleared for plantations. The British East India Company, which had its main bases further up north on the western coast, could access timber for its ships only in the forests of Kerala. Starting with trade, the region diversified into plantations and processed natural resources in the nineteenth century. Foreign enterprise was prominent in British Malabar and independent Travancore, trading in processed natural resources like tea, spices, coir rope and cashew.

At its formation (1956), Kerala had one of the highest workforce shares in non-agricultural occupations among Indian states, including in commerce and industry. In the 1970s and 1980s, a de-industrialisation and retreat from trade followed. An insular business policy suppressed some of these connections. Politics was unfriendly to foreign enterprise and sometimes hostile to private capital of any kind, even the landholding kind. Although natural resource processing and agriculture retreated, resource endowments and prehistory combined differently to create a dynamic growth story from the 1990s.

Migration and Demography

The demographic transition came here earlier than in most Indian states (Chapter 6). In the 1970s, the population growth rate was approaching near-zero after several decades of growth. There was a deep interdependence between advanced levels of literacy and healthcare on the one hand and the decline in the fertility rate on the other. Literacy encouraged going far to work, which, in turn, delayed marriage and reduced fertility.

A large literate labour force emerged in southwestern India well before 1947, owing to several things: missionary and state intervention, inter-community competition to educate, social movements, the possibility of depressed caste people seeking work outside traditional channels, and the declining political and economic power of the traditional landholders. Since long before 1947, workers from the region had been crossing borders. Certain professions like nursing and office employment drew in migrants from the area in all the big cities of India. That the opportunity to work in the Persian Gulf states would be readily seized by people from this state was consistent with this long-term propensity. The depressed state of the non-agricultural economy in the 1970s added to the impetus to go abroad.

Although emigration was going on for some time and the state had ancient links with the Arabian Sea world, emigration to the Gulf states on the scale in which it began to happen was unprecedented and a unique phenomenon. Emigration was not always cheap, and the process stimulated borrowing to finance emigration. It was also the beginning of a process of 'human integration' with the world economy and a transformation from a hitherto commodity-based integration.[18] Remittances changed consumption and investment patterns, increased regional inequality, and raised tensions between migrants and settled households and old and new economic elites. These subjects have been studied extensively, most notably by the Centre for Development Studies in 1998, 2003, 2007 and 2008 and the more recent *Kerala Migration Surveys*. The extensive scholarship also considered the prehistory of the emigration, noting that the state's higher educational levels had been a positive factor.

It is less well known that the enormous migration boom slowed from the 1990s, and while migration continued to rise in absolute numbers, the growth rate decelerated significantly. In recent years, other regions, especially Uttar Pradesh, have forged ahead of Kerala as the largest exporter of India's people. On average, the people of the state significantly increased consumption of services, rather than exporting them, and the state received people from all over India who supplied these.

While it started with the export of semi-skilled labour, the Gulf boom in its maturity was a very different thing. It led to significant capital inflow – into tourism and skilled services, and some conventional and unconventional industries. Later migrants were significantly more skilled and more specialised than the earlier ones. Many were going further afield, to Europe and North America. These new connections contributed to business development in twenty-first-century Kerala. In new businesses, value was added by accessing niche export markets or using new technologies. Natural resource extraction, for example, does not anymore mean plantations packaging harvested spices but the extraction of nutraceuticals. Jewellery manufacture involves invention and experimentation with designs. Rubber products diversified from automotive tyres to surgical accessories. Foreign investment inflow, which supported business development in princely states in the region, revived simultaneously via the Gulf and information technology routes. In short, a crude form of resource advantage matured into a reconstitution of skill-based capability.

It is a truism that politics and ideologies played a significant role in these changes. But what role? When one thinks of state politics, one thinks of a

---

[18] K. Ravi Raman, 'In-Migration vs Out-Migration', in *Mass Migration in the World-System: Past, Present and Future*, ed. Terry-Ann Jones and Eric Mielants, 122–43 (Abingdon: Routledge, 2010).

robust communist movement with its heart set on redistribution rather than growth. How does that fact square with the capitalist resurgence?

Politics and the State

A unique leftist and reformist heritage removed many barriers to labour mobility in the long run while overseeing a decentralisation of public governance in recent decades. Leftist movements began in India with a universal economic programme that was pro-worker and anti-capital. In almost all regions, the leftist parties had their main bases in rural areas. Over time, the left parties became regionalised and represented local issues of development, collaborating with urban capitalists to pursue the state's larger economic interests. In part, their record of driving foreign and big business out of the state (in both Kerala and West Bengal) returned to haunt them and led to a retreat from the old-style socialist agenda.

To understand the heritage of left politics, it is necessary to return to land. At its formation, the agricultural system was characterised by a close interdependence between land and caste. The caste Hindus (the upper castes) owned the most land, and the workers belonging to the Dalit and backward castes suffered acute deprivation and poverty. The left movement emerged in the backdrop of, and drew its energy from, social movements battling these inequalities. When leftist parties first acquired power in 1957, they promised land and educational reforms. For decades, the goodwill of the main communist party rested on these programmes. But with agriculture as a livelihood retreating, class politics could not sustain its relevance.

From the turn of the twenty-first century, a different leftist agenda took shape in the state. Class-based politics receded into the background. A new thrust on attracting investment and decentralisation emerged to the fore. The development of local self-government institutions since adopting the 73rd amendment to the Indian constitution in 1992, which empowered local bodies, has been another milestone in the legacy of the communist government in the state. With the introduction of 'People's Planning' in the mid-1990s, people's active participation in local planning was taken further.

The left legacy and business growth reinforced one another. The state is a model among Indian states of a relatively non-corrupt way of using public funds for welfare. The redistributive institutions and the tradition of participatory democracy are strong and locally rooted. These institutions have not mitigated rising inequality but have often devised countermeasures. After 1990, capitalism's resurgence restored the balance between the pursuit of welfare and the pursuit of profit, as income growth strengthened the budget and made its social policy sustainable. More ominously, however, it improved the state's creditworthiness, potentially leading to an unsustainable debt burden.

This is our story. It has a lesson.

The Lesson

Our reading of the economic history is, quite simply, that Kerala lost and rediscovered its comparative advantage. It is not an unmixed success story. The growth resurgence since the 2000s has brought enormous pressures on the environment and infrastructure. The unique natural resource endowments of the state are under threat. Devastating floods in 2018 and a near-disaster in 2019 were partly due to excessive construction in vulnerable areas and partly due to neglecting environmental management to pursue investment.[19] Similar problems appear in urban expansion, especially near the vulnerable coastlines. Growth has also bypassed many communities and increased inequality. Indeed, the state now has one of the highest levels of consumption inequality among Indian states.

From early in the twentieth century, expansion in cultivation and settlements led to a rapid loss of forest cover. The area under forests was estimated at 44 per cent of the total geographical area in 1905. It declined to 7–10 per cent in 1983. The loss of forests resulted in landslides and soil erosion, which had been accelerated by the introduction of crops such as tapioca in the hilly areas. Rainfall had declined since the 1960s, making drought risk an additional cost for farming operations.

And finally, although private sector education and healthcare have expanded, indeed been a handmaiden of leftist regimes, from long neglect, the quality of higher and technical education remains abysmal in the state. No wonder the state has a problem of educated unemployment, though debates exist on how serious that is.

---

[19] K. Ravi Raman, 'Ecospatiality: Transforming Kerala's Post-flood Riskscapes', *Cambridge Journal of Regions, Economy and Society* 13, no. 2 (2020): 319–41.

This, in broad outline, is the book's agenda. It is appropriate to start with an overview of economic change in the centuries before independence, as the regions that would later form Kerala state were drawn more firmly into emerging global commercial and political exchanges.

2

Before Independence

In the early nineteenth century, the region was ruled by three main political entities: the British Indian district of Malabar belonging to the Madras Presidency, Cochin state, and Travancore state. This was what the southwestern coast's political map looked like for 150 years before the three units were merged to form Kerala (1956). Despite this difference in political form, the three units experienced rather similar forces of change since the nineteenth century, such as the commercialisation of farming and plantations that expanded into new land frontiers, the influx and mobility of capital, labour migration, social movements targeting harsh inequalities and the decline of landholder power.

This chapter will describe the change and its legacies in the mid-twentieth century. It is helpful to start with the eighteenth century, when the political balance faced new challenges before settling down.

Trade and Politics in the Eighteenth Century

A serious European engagement with the southwestern coast of India began with Portuguese explorations in the late fifteenth century.[1] From much before, Malabar traded with West Asia and Africa. 'Nowhere in India,' wrote D. M. Dhanagare, 'have foreign trading and commercial and religious

---

[1] Ashin Das Gupta, *Malabar in Asian Trade, 1740–1800* (New York: Cambridge University Press, 1967).

interests interacted within the indigenous socio-economic and political institutions more intimately than they have in Malabar.'[2]

The chief exports of Malabar in early modern trade were spices and timber. Teak was abundantly available. A large shipbuilding industry developed, dependent on the custom of local ship-owning merchants. Beypur was the principal port in Malabar, where much of the commercial and shipbuilding activity was concentrated. In 1498, the Portuguese mariner Vasco da Gama landed in Malabar. A subsequent Portuguese attempt to impose a licensing system on coastal trade produced intermittent conflicts with the ruler of Calicut (Kozhihode), his allies inland, and a resistance force created by the Muslim merchants operating in the seaboard. The Portuguese attempt failed in the end, and the centre of Portuguese settlement shifted further north.

The cosmopolitanism of Malabar strengthened further in the second half of the eighteenth century under two forces, one maritime and another inland. In the seventeenth century, Dutch and English traders arrived to take a share of the lucrative spice trade. Portuguese influence along the Malabar coast declined in the 1660s following a war with the Dutch. The Dutch had a foothold in Ponnani, a seaboard town on the border of Cochin and Calicut.[3] With Portuguese defeat in 1663, the Dutch came to control a string of seaboard towns, the most crucial for trade being Cochin. English traders, by contrast, stayed less political and had a relatively minor presence in the port town of Tellicherry (Thalassery), 30 miles north of Calicut. Migration of merchants from Persia and Arabia, Muslims and Jews, to Calicut and other trading points after Afghan occupation of Persia in 1722 reinforced the cosmopolitanism of these settlements.

The Mysore warlord Hyder Ali's forays into Malabar from the 1760s threatened to upset the balance of power in the region. The expansion of Mysore westward drove Malabar, Cochin, Travancore and the Dutch and the British East India Companies to form military alliances.

[2] D. N. Dhanagare, 'Agrarian Conflict, Religion and Politics: The Moplah Rebellions in Malabar in the Nineteenth and Early Twentieth Centuries', *Past and Present* 74 (1977): 112–41, 112.

[3] Mahmood Kooria, 'Politics, Economy and Islam in "Dutch Ponnāni," Malabar Coast', *Journal of the Economic and Social History of the Orient* 62, no. 1 (2019): 1–34.

The kingdom of Cochin was a militarily weak power, sharing that limited power with regional warlords. Dutch protection was necessary for their survival. If the Dutch had any ambition to extend territorial control, that was restrained by the presence of two powerful states to the north and south, Calicut and Travancore. Their main business, the export of spices, depended on cooperation from the zamorin, the ruler of Calicut, but the relationship between the zamorin and the Dutch went through ups and downs. With the rise of Cochin, Ponnani lost its economic significance. The town was the last refuge of the zamorin in 1766 when Hyder Ali attacked Malabar. Refusing to pay tribute, the zamorin committed suicide.

The attempt by the Mysore state to expand its control and revenue base towards the western seaboard in the 1760s introduced a significant force of change in that it exposed the agricultural interior, and landlords settled there, to radically new political pressures. Hyder Ali wanted to control the seaboard to consolidate his power, provide protection to his friends, the French in Mahé, raise revenues, and check the possible westward advance of the Carnatic, a state in the eastern seaboard. The move, however, drew Travancore and the British into the conflict.

Cochin state was not a militarily strong force, though possessing seaports. But Travancore was an ascending power. Under Raja Martanda Varma, who had established a royal monopoly on pepper trade and production, it consolidated fiscal and military power considerably. It still needed alliances to defend itself against Mysore. A few British entrepreneurs had settled in Malabar in search of trade in aromatic spices to start with. The British joined the conflict as an ally of two states, Carnatic and Travancore, and to protect their trading interests in Tellicherry.

Nervous about Ali's designs, Travancore offered shelter to dispossessed warlords and farmers from the north who had fled the Mysorean invasion and then resisted it from strongholds. Travancore encouraged them to regroup and attack, offered the services of troops to the British in their campaigns against Mysore, and reinforced natural defences. The move to secretly buy two Dutch forts provoked a confrontation with Tipu Sultan, Hyder Ali's son and successor.

Between 1784 and 1790, Mysore and the ruler of Calicut shared territorial control of Malabar. But towards the end of 1790, Tipu Sultan withdrew. The Dutch colony in Cochin (Kochi) ended during the Napoleonic wars (1795), though most Indo-Dutch settlers stayed on. Eventually, after the third Anglo-Mysore war of 1792, the Company took over the territory formerly occupied by Mysore and Calicut. There were now two main political-economic units in the region, Travancore and British Malabar.[4]

Travancore was the southernmost state that formed the territory of Kerala. Small in territorial extent, it was one of the larger princely states around 1941. Ruled continuously by a single family from the seventeenth century onwards, the kingdom was relatively prosperous compared to an average British Indian province or some of the larger states, measured by tax collection per person or square mile. Still, the prolonged conflict with Mysore drained the state of both money and independence to consolidate its power. In the early nineteenth century, it became a vassal state of British India.

The relationship between the Travancore court and the Madras government of the East India Company was not particularly cordial. The state paid protection money, a payment the court resented. At the same time, the Company had friends inside the court who saw both economic and military advantages from the relationship. From the British point of view, a crisis developed in 1808–09 when the chief minister of the court, Velayuthan Thampi, secretly negotiated with Cochin, disaffected soldiers, French mercenaries and possibly a few American mercenaries to build a common front against the British. In 1809, he was defeated. The king signed a peace treaty, declaring Thampi a traitor. Thampi is thought to have advised the king to do this, the last ministerial action before he committed suicide. After this incident, the Company kept a strict watch on the military capability of the state, and no further threat developed to its influence on the west coast.

In territorial extent, population and size of economy, Cochin was a much smaller unit than Malabar and Travancore. In the early eighteenth century, the Dutch trading station protected it, but not very securely. The Dutch settlement was possibly the largest on Indian soil, and while its primary interest was trade in pepper, it functioned like a mini-state reliant on taxes and military service provided by locals – a many-sided process Anjana Singh calls 'localization'.[5]

Dutch protection was not enough in the 1760s when a threat came from the Samudri Raja, or zamorin, in the north. With the help of the

---

[4] On transition to colonial rule in southwestern India, more details can be had from Tirthankar Roy, *An Economic History of India, 1707–1857* (Abingdon: Routledge, 2021).

[5] Anjana Singh, *Fort Cochin in Kerala, 1750–1830: The Social Condition of a Dutch Community in an Indian Milieu* (Leiden and Boston: Brill, 2010).

Dutch and Travancore, Cochin managed to recover some of the lost lands. In the 1760s, the political situation changed dramatically as Hyder Ali's forces swooped on Malabar and threatened Cochin and Travancore. Cochin bought peace for itself by paying in money and elephants. The relationship with Mysore was still unhappy because Tipu Sultan believed rebels against his rule found shelter in Cochin and Travancore. After Tipu's exit, the British left Cochin nominally independent upon a promise to pay protection money. Relationships between the British and the rulers of Cochin were never amicable. Still, the influence of British India and its administration on the court's policies grew in the nineteenth century, when the rulers of Cochin made legislative reforms along the lines of British India.

Further into the nineteenth century, interstate conflicts died down. By the 1850s, the relationship between the British and Travancore was still troubled over allegations of corruption and mismanagement in state affairs, but no serious conflicts emerged. The rule of Rama Varma III from 1860, and the stewardship of prime minister T. Madhava Rao, made the relationship much friendlier. After 1850, economic change followed a pattern that lasted decades in all three regions. In that pattern, external trade, foreign investment, natural resource extraction and reforms in landed property rights figured prominently.

Let us start with the last topic, land rights.

Agriculture and Landed Property

Conflicts and the rise and decline of Mysorean power affected the distribution of land rights. In common with many other parts of India, in the early years of British rule in Malabar, land rights were well defined, hereditary and secure when land was held by specific castes supplying military or priestly service to the state (Nayars and Nambudris, respectively). Although not formally ownership rights, landholding rights did get sold occasionally, and increasingly on the eve of the 1792 Anglo-Mysore war. Mysore's control of Malabar had a long history, but a serious effort to govern the territory by reforming its fiscal system had to await Tipu Sultan's short-lived regime. As he tried to extract more taxes from landholders, some hereditary landholders fled to Travancore. Tipu's principal local allies, the Mappila traders and warlords, resisted the reforms. When Mysore handed Malabar over to the

British, the regime invited the old landholders back and, for decades, had to deal with conflicting claims to landholding.

While settling these rights, the British redefined landholding rights as ownership, converting inferior user rights to tenancy, an idea gaining ground and tried in Bengal at about the same time. There were two distinct drivers behind the move – promoting markets in land and investment in land, anticipating which more revenue would be taken, and creating an ally among landholders to neutralise the warlords who had served the precolonial states. Not much land improvement or sales followed, however. The impartibility of family inheritance was one obstacle. Specifically, Nayar property was usually entailed (that is, not possible to be sold after the owner's death).[6]

But the move did reinforce inequality. Landholding was probably more concentrated, and a bigger proportion of the agricultural population engaged in wage labour than in the rest of Kerala in the nineteenth century. Landlords were reportedly readier than before to eject tenants or pressure them to yield more rent. Those who found themselves in the position of tenants or under-tenants were not a homogeneous class. They were quite diverse by region and subsidiary occupation, which made resistance to these moves weak.

Among them were the Muslims, who formed about a third of the population in 1911. The Mappilas, who had settled near the seaboard, were originally traders. Some former military families settled in the interior had turned into landlords. Most members of the community and the larger Muslim population were poor tenants or under-tenants of Hindu landlords. The composition of the Muslim population in Malabar changed in the nineteenth century with the conversion of agricultural labourers in large numbers. The Slavery Abolition Act (1843) made the social status of the labouring castes more insecure than before, because not all employers were willing to pay wages to hire the same workers as before, and encouraged conversion where that improved the chances of diversifying occupations or approaching another prospective employer. The poorer sections of Muslim society, whose ranks swelled with conversion, faced a struggle after the property rights reforms.

Those who had done military service before or had a link to it and therefore owned arms but had a weak tenancy right or not even that rebelled

---

[6] On restrictions on sale, see Susan Thomas, 'Judicial Interventions and Changes in the Malabar "Nair Taravads" during the Colonial Period', *Proceedings of the Indian History Congress, 2000–2001* 61 Part I (2000–01): 945–53.

against Nayar landlords. There were several of these episodes in the early nineteenth century, followed by a disarmament and a lull that lasted until the end of the century.

Towards the end of the century, an emerging landed middle class used the courts to consolidate their position as superior tenants. That class included both Hindus and Muslims. At the same time, religion and religious institutions supplied another way to collectivise among the poorer sections of Muslim society. Historic grievances about the deprivation of land rights mattered. But Islamic revivalist sentiment was also involved, which enabled leading voices in these movements 'to cast each challenge to British power during the 19th and early 20th centuries in Islamic terms'.[7] These sentiments joined together in 1921 to cause the most serious of these incidents.

Although anti-British in sentiment, the roots of the rebellion remain disputed. Grievances around tenancy contributed to its making. Yet the fact that poor Muslims joined it in larger numbers than Hindus raises the question of whether it was mainly a peasant uprising or an Islamic revivalist movement. The rebellion did leave a legacy. A 1930 tenancy act protected tenants' rights against landlords, though it left many types of sub-tenancies outside its scope. That omission encouraged some to join left political movements to demand rights.

Like in Malabar, in Travancore the state intervened in redefining land rights. Tenants of the state held almost three quarters of the cultivated land, the remaining lands being under customary tenure held by the upper castes. In 1865, the state made the former tenancies equivalent to private proprietary rights. The move had far-reaching implications because the state's tenants were socially diverse and included many depressed caste people. The move also, and significantly, signalled an equivalence between state law and British Indian law on landed property.

From the scant historical scholarship available on the economic history of the state, it would seem that the land tenure system in Cochin was not fundamentally different from Travancore, being a mixture of state rights and superior heritable private rights.[8] But only a small part of the territory being cultivable, Cochin state was significantly less land-dependent and earned its

---

[7] Conrad Wood, 'The Moplah Rebellion of 1921–22 and Its Genesis' (PhD dissertation of School of Oriental and African Studies, London, 1975), 215.

[8] B. A. Prakash, 'Agrarian Kerala, Down the Centuries', State and Society 5, no. 1 (1984): 61–84.

income from transit taxes and taxes on salt and tobacco to a large extent. These taxes were crucial revenue sources for Travancore as well.

By comparison with north India, all three regions were much less land-dependent regarding taxation and livelihoods. The non-agricultural activities grew faster as the region was drawn into transactions with the world market. From the late nineteenth century until the mid-twentieth, the region saw growth and consolidation of private enterprise in commercial farming and in trade, processing and financing of natural resources for export.

Business

The business history before independence is much richer with Malabar and Travancore, partly because both regions received foreign investment, and much thinner on Cochin. As a trading hub, Cochin had a natural advantage, a port, and numerous waterways, extended in some cases by canal construction. A considerable part of the export trade of the western coast passed through Cochin port.[9] Large European-owned trading firms (like Aspinwall) set up bases there in the nineteenth century. In the second half of the nineteenth century, Cochin state leased out land in the hills to coffee and rubber planters, mainly Europeans, though a few were Indians. However, the forested uplands from which some of the most successful traded goods in the late nineteenth century came – spices, tea, timber, rubber and others – were more extensive in Malabar and Travancore, on which the rest of this section concentrates.

The major economic force of change in colonial Malabar was the expansion of commercial cultivation. Cultivating land to produce food grain for local and household consumption was a major occupation. Still, relative to the rest of India, more important was land that could grow commercial products – pepper, ginger, coconuts, cashew nuts, cardamom, areca nut, tapioca and banana. These crops yielded more money than did rice. Commercialisation in the rest of India would mean more grain production for the market. In Malabar, it meant more production of tree crops and spices. Commonly called 'garden' land, as opposed to wetlands for paddy,

[9] P. Ibrahim, 'The Development of Transport Facilities in Kerala: A Historical Review', *Social Scientist* 6, no. 8 (1978): 34–48.

garden cultivation expanded faster than did wetlands in the late nineteenth century. The two types were about equal in extent around 1900.

Malabar's forests and forest fringes have been famous for spices and hardwood for centuries. The exploitation of these resources for profit expanded greatly from the nineteenth century onwards. In the hills, plantations emerged. In the early nineteenth century, the state and European entrepreneurs recognised the prospect of expanding commercial cultivation in the Wayanad hills east of Calicut. A substantial plantation enterprise emerged, producing tea and coffee.

In Malabar, the British began to regulate and license timber trade soon after their political authority was established over the region. Timber extraction rights had been distributed informally before, and these rights were contested during Tipu's occupation. The British solved these complex matters by assuming the overlordship of forests and then confirming the role of the former merchants and workers in the system. Direct intervention either in the felling operations or in the trade using complicated modes of transporting logs was beyond the state, and even the European operators. Local merchants were in a strong position. As the contracts continued, members of the administration became aware of the potential dangers to the forests from unchecked extraction. In the 1820s, a contest between the conservationists and those in favour of helping the timber-starved shipping industry in Bombay ended with the former going into retreat. The licensing ended 'with devastating consequences for the Malabar forests'.[10] In the second half of the century, timber was in demand for the railways, and much of the product came from forests in Malabar until conservation rules were reinforced. Increasingly, timber was exported to Europe, making a part of the economy exposed to price fluctuations in the European markets.

Most garden lands were used as family farms. In the 1930s and 1940s, a stream of Syrian Christian migration from Travancore to Malabar's foothills encouraged crop cultivation there. With the church's help, they acquired secure rights to so-called wastelands and paddy lands and converted these into plots growing rubber, cashew, coconut, areca nut and pepper. They were

---

[10] Michael Mann, 'Timber Trade on the Malabar Coast, c. 1780–1840', *Environment and History* 7, no. 4 (2001): 403–25, 418.

people of small means and suffered disease and backbreaking hard work to make the move worthwhile.[11]

Commercialisation stimulated trade and banking. Malabar was more reliant on long-distance trade in the late nineteenth century than any other district of British India, the port cities excluded. The value of trade for domestic and export consumption grew manifold in the second half of the nineteenth century, and a new synergy developed between commerce and landholding. While the prospect of quick and high returns encouraged some traditional tenure holders to demand rent increases, it also changed the composition of the landholders. 'The new situation attracted professionals and merchants who were prepared to invest money in land, expecting high returns.'[12] Garden land, like plantation estates, became a field for capitalistic enterprise.

These shifts in capital corresponded to shifts in labour and encouraged wage labour growth as opposed to forced and caste-bound labour obligations. The population grew at a positive rate throughout the nineteenth century, accelerating in the twentieth century. Population growth added to the pool of available labourers, stimulating the clearing of forest lands for the expansion of commercial cultivation and plantations under European ownership. British planters leased land in the sparsely populated hills to grow tea, coffee, pepper and rubber.

The reformist Travancore king Rama Varma welcomed foreign investment and removed state monopolies on certain trades to encourage investment. Europeans moved into the export trade in natural-resource-based industries like coir and coconut oil. Travancore landholders produced these commodities, processed them and sold them to European trading firms. The regime at the same time centralised administration and invested money in infrastructure like roads and post offices. Land acquisition and labour contract laws in the British Indian model helped European planters procure workers and buy estate land.

Wayanad in the north had already shown the possibilities of plantations in the hills. In Travancore, concessionary land grants were on offer at least

---

[11] John Joseph, 'Peasant Migration to Malabar with a Special Reference to Peravoor Settlement (1925–1970)', *Proceedings of the Indian History Congress* 69 (2008): 1178–87.

[12] K. T. Thomas, 'The Commercialisation of Agriculture and 19th Century Agrarian Relations in Malabar', *Proceedings of the Indian History Congress* 58 (1997): 668–76.

from 1845. Tea plantation companies extensively used the offer in the last quarter of the nineteenth century. Thus, a large complex of Indo-European business linked to overseas trade emerged. It is possible, though the evidence is thin, that slavery tied to rice cultivation was seen as an obstacle to labour supply to the new enterprises.[13]

In common with Malabar, Travancore licensed timber extraction and trade and collected a great deal of money from forest produce more generally. Again, as in Malabar, the trade and felling were in the hands of indigenous merchants. In all three regions, sawmills were started to process some of the wood coming in. The earliest of these enterprises was a European venture near Beypur. In the late twentieth century, sawmills and wood processing were major fields of private investment in central Kerala.

At the turn of the nineteenth century, the threat of warfare receded from Travancore, and the state could consider schemes for revenue growth, which would mean clearing and resettling lands for cultivation. A general outcome of these interventions was the strengthening of property rights of owners, sometimes tenants, and the entry of new groups such as the Syrian Christians into landholding. From this base, some of these landed families would diversify into business.[14]

Business growth in the colonial era was essentially based on the export of commodities. Between 1870 and 1939, the value of exports from Travancore increased tenfold, corresponding to about a three-to-fourfold increase in trade volume. Reforms in commercial law, removal of monopolies, growth of the railways and an influx of European capital into trade and plantations were the foundations of this boom. None of these things the state initiated on its own. Instead, princely states, where they could, followed British India in measures taken to encourage the commercialisation of agricultural commodities. They had little choice in the matter, but these steps promised and did deliver more income to them.

In the second half of the nineteenth century, the Travancore state allowed private property rights over undeveloped lands that it laid claims on. That

---

[13] K. T. Thomas, 'The Hidden Agenda in a Welfare Garb: Socio-Economic Reforms in Travancore (19th C.)', *Proceedings of the Indian History Congress* 66 (2005–06): 949–57.

[14] T. M. Thomas Isaac and P. K. Michael Tharakan, 'An Inquiry into the Historical Roots of Industrial Backwardness of Kerala: A Study of Travancore Region', working paper of Centre for Development Studies (Trivandrum), 1986.

move, driven by fiscal motives, encouraged a tendency already underway – the migration of plains farmers to the uplands. Syrian Christians were among these migrants, the leading group and sufficiently capitalised to develop plantations.[15] In the early twentieth century, the 'agrarian expansionism' of the Syrian Christians involved lowlands as well, including some areas that were reclaimed for cultivation by flood control, again a capital-intensive form of farming.[16] In the 1920s and 1930s, banks were established to finance these enterprises.

Until 1947, four types of non-agricultural enterprises flourished in the region. The first category of enterprise formed of handicrafts that processed coir ropes, cashew and ceramic tiles. A small handloom weaving industry can be added to this list. Mostly rural and household based, some of these goods did trade widely, though rarely abroad or in the rest of India. All these enterprises attracted merchant capital. But before 1947, such firms in the traditional industry were primarily local and not individually large enterprises.

The second category consisted of plantations of tea and coffee. The tea and coffee plantation firms were mainly foreign owned, the largest being the multi-division managing agency James Finlay. European entry into tree crops had a long prehistory. However, on a serious scale, entry started from the 1880s onwards.[17] Most businesses involved corporate firms and partnerships under the managing agency system. Foreign capital with access to cheaper financial markets and personnel abroad and the joint stock limited liability rule capitalised the industry and saved on management and marketing costs. Thanks to their branches, associates and membership in auction houses in London, foreign firms were well placed to market tea in Europe and the Americas. These were high-profit-high-dividend companies and had an advantage over indigenous firms, because they had access to a global network

---

[15] P. K. Michael Tharakan, 'Dimensions and Characteristics of the Migration of Farmers from Travancore to Malabar, 1930–50', *Journal of Kerala Studies* 5, no. 2 (1978): 287–89.

[16] We borrow the phrase from Seena Devassy, 'Wealth and Social Assertion: A Study on the Self-Assertion Movements of Syrian Christians, 1900–1950', *Proceedings of the Indian History Congress* 75 (2014): 798–807.

[17] Joshy Mathew, 'Plantation Economy in Colonial Malabar – With Special Reference to Wayanad', *Proceedings of the Indian History Congress* 67 (2006–07): 730–37.

among the European groups. Networks did occasionally breed restrictive and collusive practices, especially in the 1940s.[18]

James Finlay had its own marketing system, complete with financiers and selling agents. But a great deal of tea and coffee were also marketed through the agency of another prominent multinational firm, Harrisons and Crosfield. Tea estates, of course, were large operations, which usually separated the trading and the production sides.[19] Another foreign trading firm, Aspinwall, exported spices (and timber), while also supplying shipping services to other trading firms. William Goodacre was a London-based coir mat manufacturing and exporting firm that set up a base in Cochin. An Irish-American enterprise, Darragh Smail and Co., had entered coir mat exports from Cochin and Alleppey (Alappuzha) in the late nineteenth century.

In the Wayanad uplands of Malabar, European enterprises had started in the late eighteenth and early nineteenth centuries, processing spices and producing tea, coffee, cinchona and rubber. Later, tea estates expanded faster than other businesses. As in Travancore, European trading firms Peirce Leslie and Parry were significant players in organising the export trade.[20] Rubber plantations and spice estates also attracted Europeans. But in these areas, the plantations were smaller than in tea, and many indigenous families were engaged in rubber and spices. Both commodities were traded widely, and European trading firms had a strong presence in the spice trade. Indigenous capitalists produced nearly all the coir for mats and worked as agents of European trading firms.

The third category was banking. Because agriculture was partly based on the more capital-intensive tree crops, unlike the rest of India, lending money to the families that owned such assets was relatively low risk. Kerala (and South Canara to the north, where banking flourished) had a more benign climate than northern India and did not suffer droughts and harvest failures

---

[18] K. Ravi Raman, 'Business, Ethnicity, Politics and Imperial Interests, UPASI', *Business History Review* 88, no. 1 (2014): 73–95; K. Tharian George, 'The Crisis of the South Indian Tea Industry: Legacy of the Control by British Tea Multinationals', working paper of Centre for Development Studies (Trivandrum), 1984.

[19] K. Ravi Raman, *Global Capital and Peripheral Labour: The History and Political Economy of Plantation Workers in India* (Abingdon: Routledge, 2010).

[20] W. K. M. Langley, *A Century in Malabar: The History of Peirce Leslie and Co. Ltd. 1862–1962* (Madras: Associate Printers, 1962); Hilton Brown, *Parry's of Madras: A Story of British Enterprise in India* (Madras: Parry & Co., 1954).

to the same degree. Therefore, lending to farms was a safer business here. Numerous moneylending firms and households did this business and, on the side, did some deposit and saving business. From this well-developed base, there emerged a few corporate banks.

The most famous of these enterprises, the Travancore National and Quilon Bank, started in 1937. K. C. Mammen Mappillai and most of his associates involved in establishing the bank came from the Syrian Christian community, mainly based in Travancore.[21] Literate and landowners, they were denied easy entry into the Travancore government service. Therefore, members of the community moved more into commercial agriculture, trade and finance. Syrian Christian families invested money in agriculture in lowlands and reclaimed lands (see earlier), which was capital intensive. Some held rubber-growing land or land suitable for rubber. The families followed sole proprietorship in succession and holding of property, which stimulated a land market and mortgage market more than in the case of jointly held estates common in some parts of northern India.

In the interwar period, some Syrian Christian business families pooled capital and established several large-scale enterprises. Mammen Mappillai inherited a newspaper concern and diversified into finance and industry. He also contemplated shipping. The bank had a stormy career, having run afoul of the prime minister, or *dewan*, of Travancore state. But corporate banking took root, and similar enterprises started later, often with significant participation of the Syrian Christians.

Large-scale enterprise was community-bound because of a community-based integration of commodity production, trade and finance. For that very reason, other communities, and Christians of various denominations, some based in Cochin state, 'did not want to be outdone' and entered similar businesses, especially finance, in the interwar years.[22]

The fourth category of enterprises consisted of public sector and public-sponsored ones. In the early twentieth century, the government of Travancore became interested in industrial development and targeted some small-scale craft-based industries, such as handloom textiles, for the purpose. The policy later changed and started to favour large factories. Three types of impetus

---

[21] M. J. Koshi, *K.C. Mammen Mappillai* (Trivandrum: Kerala Historical Society, 1976).
[22] M. A. Oommen, 'Rise and Growth of Banking in Kerala', *Social Scientist* 5, no. 3 (1976): 24–46, 36.

were behind the industrialisation drive: public opinion, top-down ideological shifts, and the growth of hydroelectric power.

The *dewan* (1936–47), C. P. Ramaswamy Iyer, wanted to develop the natural economic resources of Travancore, partly to augment state revenues. Other prominent Indian princely states contemplated industrialisation under state leadership in the interwar years, but all were constrained by limited access to cheap capital markets abroad. There was no legal barrier to them borrowing abroad, but most knew their bonds would not sell abroad without the guarantee of the Government of India, and the latter flatly refused to accommodate. In Iyer's time, raising finance through state–private collaboration had become a little easier to plan. Using that option, the government set up a fertiliser plant. Factories producing titanium oxide, paper and viscose fibres or rayon also started with direct or indirect state participation.[23]

Throughout the emergence of modern business, finance remained distinct and apart from industry. Finance, including corporate banks, had closer ties with land and trade. Large-scale industries raised capital and working capital in other ways. The foreign trading firms had access to the London money market or a partnership abroad; the government used taxpayers' money or, in one case, American investors; and the few indigenous industrial ventures relied on trading profits and stayed small.

Such was the story of capital engaged in industry and services. What about land and labour? The decline of old landholders and the growth of new sites of wage employment were among the several factors that laid the basis for a social revolution.

Inequality and Labour

In common with many other areas of European colonial expansion, where outright slavery had been outlawed, indigenous forms of forced and

---

[23] See also K. T. Ram Mohan, 'Material Processes and Developmentalism: Interpreting Economic Change in Colonial Tiruvitamkur, 1800–1945' (PhD dissertation submitted to the Centre for Development Studies, 1996); Raman Mahadevan, 'Industrial Entrepreneurship in Princely Travancore:1930–47', in *The South Indian Economy, Agrarian Change, Industrial Structure, and State Policy c. 1914–1947*, ed. Sabyasachi Bhattacharya, Sumit Guha, Raman Mahadevan, Sakthi Padhi, D. Rajasekhar and G. N. Rao, 159–207 (Delhi: Oxford University Press, 1991).

involuntary labour continued in Malabar long after the advent of British rule there. Confined to agricultural work, such forms of labour persisted probably because they did not resemble formal slavery but had features common to serfdom. Conditions were not very different in Travancore. In most cases, the so-called slave was attached to a plot of land. Sometimes, but not usually, they were sold apart from the land. The number of such workers increased in the early nineteenth century as land was cleared for cash crops.[24]

Formal slavery was abolished in Malabar in 1843. In Travancore, slavery was abolished in 1853, but not before the missionaries and the British state placed considerable pressure upon the king. The king was in two minds because slaves were used extensively in paddy cultivation. Formal abolition did little to end caste-biased discrimination and repression. The population subject to such repression continued to be large. A census conducted in 1875 showed a surprisingly large proportion of the depressed caste population in the state, though this body was diverse in the degree of untouchability practised. That is, there were inequalities among the depressed caste groups. With considerable success, the missions concentrated on the most repressed groups for conversion and education.

The growth of commerce and industry, small towns, government jobs and the Christian missions combined to encourage the spread of literacy, English education, education for girls and the growth of a middle class cutting across the old courtly or landholding elite. These changes touched the lives of the depressed caste population. Whereas caste Hindus dominated government employment, others, including the depressed caste groups, joined small businesses, especially copra, coir and the liquor trade. World War I 'provided new opportunities for Travancoreans to go abroad and experience western middle-class life at first hand'.[25] That opportunity was again available to the depressed groups. In the interwar period, a strong equality and civil rights movement emerged to weaken barriers to opportunities for the depressed castes and Christians in public administration.

Workers' geographical mobility contributed to a decline in the old forms of caste-mediated inequality. The tea plantations in the hills were a major employer of workers from the depressed castes. These were wage-based and

---

[24] Sebastian Joseph, 'Slave Labour of Malabar in the Colonial Context', *Proceedings of the Indian History Congress* 45 (1984): 694–703.

[25] Robin Jeffrey, 'Temple-Entry Movement in Travancore, 1860–1940', *Social Scientist* 4, no. 8 (1976): 3–27, 11.

contractual employment governed by the law – a far cry from the brutal untouchability of the village. That wage employment would have a liberating effect contemporary administrators were aware of and hoped for. And yet the change in circumstances was less dramatic and much slower than might be hoped for. Precisely because many of the workers came from the most depressed castes, harsh conditions and low wages persisted. Planters were mini-states in their domain, which made for an arbitrary use of authority at times.[26]

Alongside these changes, the old landholding elite experienced a decline in its dominant position in the economy and society. Robin Jeffrey called the process 'the decline of Nayar dominance' in a famous book.[27] Nayar landholders and Brahmin landlords were prominent in the countryside in the nineteenth century, and their rights paralleled that of their counterparts in British Malabar. The Christian missions weakened their hold upon labour from the mid-nineteenth century onwards. The commercialising rural economy created many avenues of mobility, which the Nayars did not join in large numbers. To get ahead in life, members of the group needed to compete – in higher education, for example – with other communities. But the Nayars had no particular advantage over their side in that race.

A further reason for the decline was the attrition of the impartible inheritance principle in Nayar extended households. Some of these households were formed through descent from ancestresses. Women, however, had little say over the management of the estates, which the men managed and held together thanks to legal recognition for the joint family or impartible inheritance. The system came under attack from within by upwardly mobile individuals and reformist groups. Judges in the nineteenth century were ambivalent about the merits of departing from the joint family, held as an ideal in many parts of British India. But the pressure grew in the twentieth century. In 1933, a new law formally allowed partition.[28]

Social movements that had begun in an obscure way among communities were becoming political and concerned the state in the 1930s and the 1940s. In the field of mass education, advances had begun earlier. In the 1910s, late in the rule of Rama Varma V, the government reinforced it by significantly

---

[26] Raman, *Global Capital and Peripheral Labour*.
[27] Robin Jeffrey, *The Decline of Nayar Dominance: Society and Politics in Travancore, 1847–1908.* (New Delhi: Vikas, 1976).
[28] S. Thomas, 'Judicial Interventions'.

raising the amount of money spent on schools. Equality movements gathered pace via caste organisations.

Poor tenants found an alternative political platform, the growing socialist and communist groups. Communist sympathisers in the Madras legislature took up their cause. Incidentally, the communist movement in Bengal too was successful in drawing in tenants with weak or no legal rights. In both cases, the proliferation of sub-tenancy was not just a creation of the law but a joint outcome of an extremely limited supply of land and rapid and sustained population growth.

At the time of independence (1947), the left movement had gathered force. The Communist Party had a support base among poor farmers, especially those with weak proprietary rights. It competed with caste groups to represent the interests of the depressed caste people, predominantly wage workers. The Great Depression and the subsequent credit crisis damaged the relationship between the joint landholding households and the tenants and labourers.[29] The leadership, however, came from the educated middle class with ties to the nationalist movement.

The Stride in Mass Education

The dramatic growth of literacy in the state across the caste divide happened because of several economic and social factors, most importantly, economic mobility that did not depend on the land and the identification of mobility with education. The puzzle does not go away, however. Some of the same forces could be found elsewhere in India in the late nineteenth century, with outcomes that were similar but nowhere near as impressive in scale. At least three things made Travancore special in the backdrop of British and colonial India.

First is Christianity. Christianity in this part of India had precolonial roots in the migration of Syrian Christians or converts to Roman Catholicism by Portuguese priests in the seventeenth century. The Catholic Church had always been engaged in public welfare, though in these earlier times, its activities benefited specific communities. Along with European merchants and planters came European missions. And as they did, spirituality and

---

[29] Dilip M. Menon, *Caste, Nationalism and Communism in South India. Malabar, 1900–1948* (Cambridge: Cambridge University Press, 1994).

economic mobility became interconnected. In the nineteenth century, the protestant missions played a more revolutionary role in welfare.

Nineteenth-century Christianity is deeply connected with the history of social movements in the region. Much has been written on the role of evangelical Christian missions in promoting social reform and encouraging mobility, especially in southern India. It becomes clear from this scholarship that the missions attracted the attention of depressed and upwardly mobile groups for their efforts in education, especially English education. Missions did not always succeed as a force for conversion or in spreading mass literacy, let alone creating new employment opportunities. But where dramatic transformations did happen, the mission was present. One such success story was the London Missionary Society of southern Travancore, which set up 'an educational system for men and women of all castes and creeds, crowned by an English Seminary in Nagercoil'.[30]

As the protestant missions took the lead in education, the Catholic Church tried to catch up. It was always involved in supplying communities within its fold with some welfare goods. But the start of effective participation by the Catholic Church in supplying public goods dates to about 1900. It increased substantially later in the twentieth century. With many employers of private enterprise belonging to the Catholic Church, the Church also took part in industrial relations and disputes as a mediator and encouraged the employment of women workers because they were less unionised. That move indirectly promoted women's employment.[31]

One should not overstate the significance of mass education. It was hardly a revolutionary change at the time it unfolded. Its transformative potential was limited to mainly one factor: the ability of people from this region to migrate further away in search of more paying jobs. Education by itself did not deliver, not directly at least, either caste equality or gender equality.

---

[30] Dick Kooiman, 'The Gospel of Coffee: Mission, Education and Employment in 19th Century Travancore', *Economic and Political Weekly* 19, no. 35 (1984): 1535–44.

[31] 'Between 1965 and 1973, the Church was running more than 800 development projects throughout Kerala, including 550 hospitals; it had 840,000 students in its schools; and it received Rs. 32 million of foreign aid for development and charity work'. P. Neethi, 'Globalization Lived Locally: Investigating Kerala's Local Labour Control Regimes', *Development and Change* 43, no. 6 (2012): 1239–63, 1247.

The missions' agency is in no doubt, but the scale of their impact was probably limited because of their limited capacity. Mass education needed the government. What was the state doing?

The State

In the nineteenth century, public education was entirely sporadic and weak. Although the first government English school started (in Travancore) in 1834, there is much uncertainty about just how significant and deep the state's role was in shaping the early history of modernisation. All that the state did was sustain indigenous and vernacular schools, which not only provided education but also practised segregation. A history of education in Travancore attributes the state's advance to this factor, which gave the public education system that came later in the twentieth century a foundation to build on.[32] In the late nineteenth century, the state funded some schools and probably aided some private schools. However, private enterprise was larger in scale, and the amount of state aid was unknown.

Full-fledged public education was a later development. A law that made primary education compulsory came in very late in the story, in 1946. Pressures upon the state from below would have been weak in spite of reformers and leaders like Narayana Guru, Ayyankali and Vakkom Mohammed Abdul Khader Moulavi, who consistently asked for education access for the depressed communities. As in British India, an elected legislature began in 1919, and the old land tenure holders dominated the limited franchise. From the interwar period, the state's role enlarged not only in funding mass education but also in higher education and teacher training. By then, the state's unusual trajectory in mass literacy had been established.

In making sense of this success story of mass education, especially when set against the unimpressive record of British India, one narrative comes readily to mind: Enlightened independent princes minded welfare more than the British colonial rulers, who neglected it. This narrative does not quite work because the state led the process only in the twentieth century. And

---

[32] P. K. Michael Tharakan, 'Socio-Economic Factors in Educational Development: Case of Nineteenth Century Travancore', *Economic and Political Weekly* 19, no. 45 (1984): 1913–28.

when it did join the process, something other than an enlightened mindset was at work. This was superior fiscal capacity.

Whereas most British Indian districts relied on taxes collected from poor peasants living on land that yielded too little per capita output, some southern states like Travancore had a different economic structure and scored significantly more success in raising revenue. To see what difference fiscal capacity made, compare Travancore's finances with those of its neighbouring Indian province, Madras, around 1901–04.[33]

Revenue/head, Madras: Rupees 1.24; Travancore: Rupees 2.71

Revenue/square mile, Madras: Rupees 340; Travancore: Rupees 1,516

Travancore had greater financial resources than neighbouring Madras. Where did this capacity derive from? Land revenue delivered about a third of Travancore's and British India's total revenue. Interestingly, one item that delivered a significantly higher tax to the Travancore state compared with British India was salt, a regressive consumption tax that British India tried to use at a considerable political cost. A princely state was presumably less susceptible to nationalist backlash. Travancore and Cochin relied heavily on an import tax on salt coming in from Bombay or Madras. Under an agreement with British India, they could do this subject to some restrictions.

Besides salt, and tobacco excise, licence fees collected from assessment of garden land, or land growing commercial tree crops, and from forest produce – a joint effect of its geography and attraction for foreign capital – delivered substantial income to the state. The combined heads yielded about 10–15 per cent of the state revenue, and nothing quite like this existed in British India. Because these other heads were available, the state could offer generous concessions to plantations and families for clearing forests for commercial cultivation, which added to the revenues in the long run.

Superior state capacity was strengthened by the fact that the Indian princes received an explicit protection guarantee from British India, meaning they did not need to spend any money on external defence. While they received an enormous implicit subsidy, British India spent an inordinate sum on its army, leaving little for public goods.

---

[33] Data from V. Nagam Aiya, *Travancore State Manual*, vol. I (Trivandrum: Travancore Government Press, 1906), 645; and Government of India, *Statistical Abstracts for British India* (London: HMSO, 1901–04).

'If the freedom of women is an index of civilization,' a census report of 1875 said, 'then Travancore is decidedly the most advanced country in the world....'[34] Was the condition of women that different in the colonial era?

Women

Matriliny and women's academic advancement in the early twentieth century were sometimes thought of as pathways to gender equality. That was far from the case. Matriliny or education did not translate, among any of the elite groups that practised matriliny, into gender equality in the matter of property inheritance. Nor were the more literate Syrian Christians particularly progressive in the matter. In fact, religion-based laws like the Christian Succession Act that the Travancore state accepted as the standard were famously unequal on property division. Because it was, dowry was common, and the amount varied with the grooms' earning power. Child marriages were common among the Muslims of Malabar, Tamil Brahmins and Malayali Brahmins in the 1930s and 1940s. The Travancore state's successful implementation of a child marriage act in the 1930s led to a spate of petitions among wealthy Hindus and Christians seeking exemptions from its provisions.

Despite stubborn conservatism, education did initiate a process of change. Because of the spread of education, the opposition to the act was relatively weak. A woman with solid schooling and English schooling would want to be less dependent on the inheritance of parental property and join the workforce as a teacher or medical professional. It is hard to measure how many unmarried women had left their homes to join services elsewhere before 1947. Biographical material suggests that the proportion, though small, was higher than among women elsewhere in India at that time.

The Protestant missions were particularly effective because of two things: making and promoting the dissemination of printed books and pamphlets and girls' education. The former enterprise was directly a result of the attempt to produce new textbooks for use in schools but indirectly contributed to the growth of printing and publishing as an industry and public libraries. Some Protestant missions were headed by a family, which was an advantage

---

[34] Cited in Anna Lindberg, 'Child Marriage in Late Travancore: Religion, Modernity and Change', *Economic and Political Weekly* 49, no. 17 (2014): 79–87.

in caring for girls. They initially often came from low-income families or were orphans and came to the schools looking mainly for a safe shelter. Later, the missions targeted girls from upper castes, adapting the plan to maintain segregation between castes.[35]

Tomila Lankina and Lullit Getachew show, with district-level data across India, colonial and postcolonial, that Protestant missionary activities encouraged women's education with a long legacy.[36] The legacy was powerful. In the long run, the missions 'pioneered co-educational, and introduced new forms of female schooling for all religious groups; female Christian converts also experienced additional educational effects in terms of literacy retention at a later age due to Church practice'.[37]

One of the first professions to employ educated women was nursing, and this was an all-India market. Health awareness, if not public health, had a precocious start in the region in the 1860s, when the Travancore kings endorsed vaccination, thus stimulating the 'elite uptake of colonial medicine' in the state.[38] In contrast, there was still considerable resistance to colonial medicine in the rest of India. In the next decade, recruitment of female nurses began in the state, but too sporadically to suggest a pattern. Nevertheless, recruitment, again an unusual development in contemporary India, led to the question: why Kerala? Here, more than the king's agency, that of the Protestant missions which became active in the region in the nineteenth century was more important.

In the 1930s, when admission of nursing students in the Christian Medical College, Vellore, in Madras Presidency, increased, most recruits were Christians from the region. This was then the largest school in south India. With an undergraduate degree in nursing on offer, Vellore produced an elite set that would later shape policy and lead institutions. In the nineteenth century, missionary activities had already aided the professionalisation of nursing. In 1943, the Travancore state started its school of nursing.

---

[35] Sam Nesamony, 'Missionaries, Literacy and Intellectual Consciousness in South Travancore', *Proceedings of the Indian History Congress*, 77 (2016): 651–64.

[36] Tomila V. Lankina and Lullit Getachew, 'Competitive Religious Entrepreneurs: Christian Missionaries and Female Education in Colonial and Post-Colonial India', *British Journal of Political Science* 43, no. 1 (2013): 103–31.

[37] Lankina and Getachew, 'Competitive Religious Entrepreneurs', 125.

[38] Sujani K. Reddy, *Nursing and Empire: Gendered Labor and Migration from India to the United States* (Chapel Hill: University of North Carolina Press, 2015), 121.

The early recruits into senior positions were often Christians, especially Christians from Kerala. The 1930s recruits in Vellore included Syrian Christians. Did religion create a selection and entry bias? It is hard to test this hypothesis directly. But it has stimulated considerable literature about the 'stigma' associated with nursing. Many orthodox Hindus from the upper castes believed in some version of untouchability or the prospect of pollution by touching another's body. That sentiment was not compatible with nursing. Interestingly, as recently as the early 2000s, the issue of stigma was still alive and still a factor shaping patterns of entry into nursing. Christians contributed significantly to the flow of migrant nurses in the Indian and overseas markets.

Religion was not the only explanation for this recruitment bias. Nursing was mainly a woman's profession, and many women would join paid work for the years between attaining adulthood and marriage. The average age at marriage mattered to this decision to work, and this age was lower in British India and among Hindus than in the princely states of the region. There were other distinctions. For example, as Robin Jeffrey notes, 'women retained a circumscribed but influential position in social life', a fact that has become transformative in the years to come.[39] These generalisations are too broad to be easily testable. Counterexamples showing persistent conservatism exist. But they suggest that women's participation in paid work had owed to deep societal features and not just external intervention.

Conclusion

Kerala, around 1900, was a region composed of three major political units. Regional politics made for some differences in economic change. For example, the state capacity to spend on public goods was significantly higher for Travancore. Still, there was a broad similarity between the three units in the pattern of economic change in 1850–1950.

Agriculture was the most prominent livelihood, but not as significant as in most other parts of India, if we mean by agriculture the production of field crops. The most profitable natural resources came from land under tree crops, yielding spices, timber, forests suitable for pulp usable in paper

---

[39] Robin Jeffrey, *Politics, Women and Well-Being: How Kerala Became a Model* (Basingstoke: Palgrave Macmillan, 1992).

and rayon, ilmenite, pottery clay, coconut fibre and derivatives, and others. These areas of the economy traded a lot more and over longer distances than would be the case with the grain trades. Both production and commerce in these activities engaged hired wage labour and foreign capital relatively more than in conventional agriculture. In turn, the internal labour market and expansion of the new land frontier encouraged the circulation of middle-class farmers (especially Syrian Christians) and members of the depressed castes within the larger region. These patterns emerged in sharp relief in the interwar period.

The states in all three regions helped foreign capital. Fundamentally, business developed using locally found natural resources rather than political favours. The fact that foreign enterprise was prominent both in British Malabar and independent Travancore suggests that colonialism was neither a negative nor a positive force in the growth of capitalism in the region.

The emergence of a literate labour force – to many, a distinct feature of southwestern India – depended on several things: the missions, inter-community competition to educate, social movements, the possibility of depressed caste people seeking work outside traditional channels, and the declining political and economic power of the traditional landholders. The state stepped into mass education late but with significantly greater resources on average than a British Indian district. It was not a marginal player but reinforced rather than scripted a social revolution that had begun earlier.

3

The Retreat of Agriculture

In 1956 (and even now), two distinct types of agriculture existed in the state: cultivation of seasonal field crops and cultivation of tree crops. The latter held steady in the long run. But traditional agriculture, especially paddy cultivation, for which the lowlands and the river basins were especially suitable, has seen a relentless decline since 1970. Twenty years into the new millennium, traditional agriculture was an insignificant employer and earner, and for most people still engaged in it, the land provided no more than a subsidiary income. A relative retreat from traditional agriculture is not news. It happened everywhere. In the state the fall was spectacular.

What was this a change from? Although agriculture employed a smaller proportion of the workforce than in India at the start of this journey, it was not a marginal livelihood. Land control secured the political power of the elites in the princely states. A variety of crops were cultivated throughout the state, from monsoon rice to tapioca, ginger, groundnut, sugarcane and pulses. Most were rarely traded outside the region but were vital to sustaining local consumption. Good croplands occurred in clusters. Because of the topography, land available for the cultivation of traditional field crops was less than half the total land area of the state. Alluvial soil occurs in a narrow strip along the coast or in river valleys. Land elsewhere is not as fertile, though frequently suitable for tree crops. Unlike in most regions of India, access to water was not a serious problem. Soil quality and drainage of excess water were bigger problems.

Good land, however, was extremely scarce relative to the population. The exceptionally high population density in the areas of cultivation ensured a level of available land per head that was a fraction of the Indian figure (0.6 acres against an Indian average of 3.1 acres around 1970) and low by any benchmark.[1] Partly, the density reflected high labour demand in lowlands to deal with drainage and seasonal flooding. Paddy yield was very high in these areas, but paddy cultivation needed a lot of people. From the 1940s, this zone in the middle was emerging as a political battleground. The leftist political parties organised the poorest of the tenants and workers into unions. Class-based movements to get higher wages, better employment terms or more land and movements to achieve equal social status often merged because the agricultural labourers came from the depressed castes. The central paddy zone was the original home of leftist politics in the state.

When in power for the second time (from 1967), the leftist parties delivered, first, a land reform that went much further than similar policies elsewhere in India and then trade union control and regulation of work and wages. What was happening on land had a deep impact upon employer–employee relationships in every other field and gathered force in the 1970s. This was the only state to implement minimum wage laws strictly. Agricultural wages rose and maintained parity with somewhat higher non-agricultural wages. At the end of the 1980s, rural wages were almost double those of neighbouring Tamil Nadu.[2]

In land, the wage revolution announced the beginning of the end of traditional agriculture. The average asset base being so small, employers were squeezed hard. Acreage cropped fell. Those who remained tied to land did so because they had nowhere to go, or they worked the land with mainly family labour. Capitalistic or commercial agriculture was dying outside the plantation sector. The first Green Revolution then unfolding in the rest of India, including Tamil Nadu, passed the state by.

There is no puzzle in the story told so far. What made all this totally anomalous was the high rate of unemployment in the countryside, possibly the highest in the country at the end of the 1960s. Apparently, high unemployment rates held steady for the next twenty years. How were high wages and the retreat of a major livelihood possible at all in this condition? How could the unions sustain their hold on the labour market? How did the leftist parties retain their hold on state politics?

---

[1] J. H. Ansari, 'A Study of Settlement Patterns in Kerala', *Ekistics* 30, no. 180 (1970): 427–35.

[2] T. N. Krishnan, 'Wages, Employment and Output in Interrelated Labour Markets in an Agrarian Economy: A Study of Kerala', *Economic and Political Weekly* 26, no. 26 (1991): A82–A96.

The combination of high wages and high unemployment that seemed to continue forever inspired scholars in the 1990s and beyond. Many research papers were published from the end of the 1990s onwards to explain the puzzle. This research effort and the other chapters in this book help us to complete the narrative. The missing elements were Gulf remittances and emigration that shaped traditional agriculture in unseen and indirect ways. Little of that money went into land or agricultural technology. But a lot of it went into potentially competing or complementary livelihoods in the same villages where agriculture was also a major occupation. That money flowed into construction, retail trade, transport, cinema halls, restaurants and shops. This emerging service sector labour market absorbed the effort of those who had been made redundant in traditional agriculture or did not want to work there anymore. Both employers and employees figured in that set. This transformation of local labour markets was poorly represented in employment data. Unemployment data was an illusion. Much later, rural non-farm employment surveys captured it better.

The fall of traditional agriculture was cushioned in this way. But that is not the whole story. The leftist movement reinvented itself and had to deal with backlash as farmers formed lobbies and joined political parties. That episode figures elsewhere in the book. The rest of the chapter returns to narrative history. A good place to start is the hub of traditional agriculture in the central lowlands before the land reforms began.

Land Reclamation and the Emergence of Capitalist Agriculture

Almost without exception, agriculture relied on the heavy rains that the southwest monsoon brought to the Malabar coast between June and September. The rains made possible paddy cultivation in the otherwise dry and lateritic areas near the Western Ghats. Wells were easy to construct in the lateritic areas, making some irrigated agriculture possible there. On the other hand, the rains made a lot of the fertile loamy soils inaccessible in the central lowlands.

In most regions of the state, the landholding pattern consisted of a mixture of peasant proprietorship and large landholders before the radical land reforms of 1969 onwards. Peasant property was nothing out of the ordinary, but the large landholders had an unusual role in history. Large landowners were usually the upper-caste Hindus with superior hereditary rights, or Hindu and

Christian moneyed people who leased in land from the former. Since 1880, they had led a large-scale conversion of swamps, marshes and lowlands susceptible to seasonal flooding into cultivable croplands (Chapter 2).

Some of the earliest projects began in the 1830s, but the pace of land reclamation picked up in the 1880s with easier financing by private moneylenders and later banking firms. Depending on the terrain and the type of water body in question, the project involved building dams, draining and pumping and, often, driving coconut stems into the bed. By the mid-twentieth century, several hundred thousand acres had been recovered from water in the Kuttanad region, by then the rice bowl of the state. Most of the land was still available for the rice cultivation season only, but it was highly fertile for that one use.[3]

Partly because of the heavy labour involved in land reclamation throughout the year, the proportion of agricultural workers was unusually high in Kuttanad, reaching as much as 50 per cent of the rural workforce in 1961. Compared with the intensive cultivation zones in the Indo-Gangetic Basin, agriculture employed less livestock per head, almost no machine power, but more human labour. That scenario changed somewhat in the 1980s, but the high labour intensity persisted. Despite the high labour demand, the high population density and oversupply of workers depressed wages enough to make it worthwhile for employers to invest money in cultivation. The legacy of caste hierarchy added further force to the inequality.

A study of paddy cultivation in Kuttanad in 1973 described how the process worked.[4] The Vembanad lake, stretching north–south for nearly 60 miles in the south-central area, carried a large part of the monsoon rainwater. With the monsoon and the excess water receding, farmers became busy working on the land still under shallow (up to about 10 feet deep) water. Where possible, they erected temporary embankments and drained the water physically. The fields were then ploughed, and sprouted seeds were broadcast upon them. By early winter and just before the northeast monsoon arrived, the fields were ready for harvest.[5]

---

[3] V. R. Pillai and P. G. K. Panikar, *Land Reclamation in Kerala* (Bombay: Asia Publishing, 1965).

[4] K. C. Alexander, 'Emerging Farmer–Labour Relations in Kuttanad', *Economic and Political Weekly* 8, no. 34 (1973): 1551–60.

[5] According to recent reports, the lake's carrying capacity has fallen in the last decade or two, risking monsoon floods.

Land Reform and Trade Union Power

A year after the formation of the state, a democratically elected communist government came to power. The government was toppled two years later, but the main communist parties remained a powerful element in state politics and returned to power in 1967, now heading a coalition. Towns in central Kerala, where industries had developed, were the nodes of communist mobilisation to begin with. Alappuzha (Alleppey) was perhaps the most important centre. Spreading out into the agricultural interior was a short step from here. When the party returned to power, its base was solid among tenants, labourers and small farmers in the lowland rice belt.

In 1969, a sweeping land reform policy was announced. Ownership rights were delivered to cultivating tenants. Those living in hutments without a secure title to that land received the title. These lands sometimes contained small plots that were cultivated or grew coconut. The reforms excluded the plantations from their scope and, while acknowledging a role for seizing land above a certain ceiling, did not implement outright redistribution. Since the 1950s, redistributive land reform had been an explicit goal of policy but delivered little real action in most states. Kerala was different. So was West Bengal ten years later, where land reform took the form of re-titling rather than redistribution. In both cases, leftist political parties were in power, and they had come to power on the promise of land reform.

The fundamental problem in both cases was the exceptionally high density of the population. There was simply not enough land to redistribute and keep agriculture viable for any landowner, old or new. In the state, given the geography, the scarcity was even more acute. And the solution inevitably created a new problem. In the presence of acute land scarcity, the land reforms turned almost every landowner into a 'marginal' farmer, able to make ends meet if exceptionally lucky and living in worse poverty if not.[6] The policy distributed poverty more evenly than before. It created many new landowners, thereby reducing the average landholding much too low. It made the business almost uneconomical for both the old and the new farming classes. On the political plane, the move disempowered the landowners significantly. Some were affiliated with the leftists. Others lost what little clout they had before. In 1967, the Kerala Land Utilization

---

[6] P. S. George, 'Emerging Trends in Size Distribution of Operational Holdings in Kerala', *Economic and Political Weekly* 21, no. 5 (1986): 198–200.

Act (1967) had prohibited the conversion of paddy land to other uses, which obstructed farmers' choices to escape the situation.

Land reforms left the poorest earners in agriculture – workers – untouched. Indeed, the employers had lost their ability to sustain profitable agriculture in many cases because of a smaller asset base. In this scenario, the trade unions stepped in with a mandate to raise wages and regulate working conditions. This was a broadly successful effort. Wages rose and stayed high forever.

It would be a mistake to think that the mobilisation succeeded because the communist supporters were poor and struggling. In Kuttanad, the poorest earners earned on average an income about half that of the landholder, lower but not significantly lower. Besides, most low earners were literate, subscribed to newspapers even when deprived of many other consumer goods, and aspired to educate their children. Their political awareness and aspirations made them a very different sort of underclass when compared with the rest of India.

In this setting, the agricultural workers' unions affiliated with the main communist parties could implement regulations on hours and wages with little resistance. Those workers who did not fall in line were treated badly, on occasion brutally. As for the landowners, their only recourse was to join an opposing political lobby and fight out their case in the ballot box. In this way, political affiliations became fragmented, a factor that was to shape state politics for years to come.

In the 1970s, trade union power was universally exercised. Wages did rise. But that rise increasingly looked like an anomaly, a puzzle, because agriculture and the landholders were beginning to do badly from then on. That was not all. As the anthropologist Joan Mencher said in articles published in the 1970s, there were significant new elements working against the sustainability of the high-wage regime. People joined agricultural labour from other professions in distress – fishermen who had lost out to mechanised trawlers and workers in closed and bankrupt cashew and coir factories who had lost their jobs because the business had shifted to Tamil Nadu.[7] At the same time, the combined effect of the land reform and wage rise was generating bitterness among landowners, large or small. Wherever she went

---

[7] Joan P. Mencher, 'Why Grow More Food? An Analysis of Some Contradictions in the "Green Revolution" in Kerala', *Economic and Political Weekly* 13, nos. 51/52 (1978): A98–A104.

(1977–78) during her surveys, she heard complaints 'about the high wages, the terrible militancy of the labourers, their insolence and lack of respect, how they would not co-operate, and how they do not understand the plight of the farmers'.[8] Universally, landholders had grown interested in shedding jobs, an almost impossible thing to do in paddy.

The countryside was not in the best of times in the 1970s. The 1970s Green Revolution, because it was wheat-based, had no chance in the state, and the 1980s Green Revolution, which was paddy-based, had no chance either because the high wage was killing paddy. Surprisingly, the countryside did not descend into an outright political or economic crisis. There were some endogenous responses to the crisis, including investment in technology. But a long-term pattern was setting in that shifted the driver of income and job growth to services, while saving rural consumption and investment from a precipitous decline. Gulf remittances, directly or indirectly, played a large role in shaping that pattern. Labour migration saved the leftists.

A 1980s Turnaround and the Long-term Pattern

The broad-based changes in the economy did not leave agriculture untouched. The decline in cropland slowed, and investment in land picked up as the second paddy-based Green Revolution was underway. Thanks to water and soil, the lowlands still promised one of the highest levels of paddy output per acre in the country. Land reforms had reduced the average holdings to tiny levels, but even these holdings yielded an income that compared well with that of small farmers and tenants in the rest of India. Land preparation in the lowlands was an extremely labour-intensive operation, and it made sense for some employers to replace labour with animal and tractor power. These changes happened, and even though trade unions restrained the extent of tractor use and technological change, the changes contributed to a positive output growth in agriculture in the 1980s.[9]

---

[8] Mencher, 'Why Grow More Food?' A102.

[9] K. P. Kannan, 'Agricultural Development in an Emerging Non-Agrarian Regional Economy: Kerala's Challenges', *Economic and Political Weekly* 46, no. 9 (2011): 64–70; K. P. Kannan and P. Pushpangadan, 'Dissecting Agricultural Stagnation in Kerala: An Analysis across Crops, Seasons and Regions', *Economic and Political Weekly* 25, nos. 35–36 (1990): 1991–2004.

In the 1980s, tenancy re-emerged in Kuttanad in clandestine forms.[10] Many landowning families had too small holdings to specialise in agriculture. On the other hand, they had access to more salaried jobs in the state or outside it. It made sense for them to lease out land to those with more limited choices. Agricultural workers leased these lands and cultivated them. Landowners feared the prospect that the tenants would stake a claim to the property and changed tenants regularly. The short contracts were a different system from older forms of tenancy that involved long-term arrangements between two families.

The 1990s and the first two decades of the new millennium saw the long-term pattern affirmed. In the long term, agriculture experienced a near-zero growth of income, even as average income growth picked up in the state. The sector was no longer the driving force behind that change in any significant sense. Exponential growth in services took over. In absolute terms, agriculture did not decline any further, but it did not matter much, if at all, to the state's economic miracle.

Traditional agriculture was still potentially a paying operation because of high paddy yields. Where possible, plantation crops expanded. But the extent of croplands growing paddy continued to fall, if slowly. More land was left fallow. More people left cultivation and joined other work. There was a deliberate withdrawal of both investment capital and labour supply from cultivation. For the employers, it was getting harder to get workers. Workers demanded wages that squeezed profits too much.

As we mentioned, research produced in the 1990s tried to answer what appeared as a paradox – high wages amidst high rates of unemployment in the village. Unemployment rates were among the highest among all Indian states. Why did workers not move around more in search of work? How was this combination sustainable at all? One obvious explanation for the high wage was trade union activity. But in the presence of unemployment, unions would have limited freedom to negotiate, and the high wage would not be sustainable anyway. Politics, which does explain the high wage, would not explain the stickiness of the high wage.

The research revealed a rural economy that was changing in extraordinary ways. One of its peculiar features was the lack of mobility. The mode of labour-use in cultivation was highly specific to local conditions. Therefore,

---

[10] K. K. Eswaran, 'Reemergence of Land Leasing in Kerala: The Case of Kuttanad', *Social Scientist* 18, nos. 11/12 (1990): 64–80.

local labour was mostly used instead of migrant workers. In fact, labour transactions occurred to a very limited extent even between neighbouring villages, in sharp contrast with the long-distance migration trend.[11] Because of limited mobility, local shortages of labour tended to persist. This was unusual in India, but it still would not explain the persistence of high wages as long as local unemployment remained high. Something was still missing.

A second peculiar feature was that the landowners and employers of labour were losing interest in the business. The land reforms had ensured that there were too many landowners owning individually too small holdings. Their capacity to absorb the costs of cultivation was limited to begin with. The costs of the management of labour in traditional agriculture were just too high.[12] If wages rose too, it made sense to invest their savings elsewhere. This sentiment was behind the re-emergence of tenancy in Kuttanad. In the long run, the pressures increased not only for the landowners but also for the tenants and workers who were leasing land. But even this factor, which does explain the retreat of traditional agriculture, would not explain the persistence of high wages.

A third piece of the puzzle was that the unemployment data was wrong. Unemployment levels are always hard to define because they reflect the perceptions of the workers about their conditions rather than real conditions. In the case of this state, data to trace how the enormous remittance flow filtered into the village was always scarce. That missing element potentially resolves the paradox. Employment and work re-emerged in ways that did not show up well in macro datasets. Only special surveys of rural non-farming work revealed the transformation.

For the workers, the persistent seasonal unemployment and, for the employers, the high costs of the operation acted as a strong push to invest in businesses outside farming, in shops, transport, or retail trade. As mentioned already, Gulf money gave a tremendous boost to private construction. All of that brought a range of non-farming employment within reach of a population that lived in the farming village and did not want to work in farming because it paid little to do so. In this way, in the 1980s, the state emerged as a high-wage economy with the highest incidence among all

---

[11] M. K. Sukumaran Nair, 'Rural Labour Market in Kerala: Small Holder Agriculture and Labour Market Dynamics', *Economic and Political Weekly* 32, no. 35 (1997): L45–L52.

[12] Sukumaran Nair, 'Rural Labour Market'.

Indian states of rural non-farm employment. The leftist unions could sustain their power to regulate wages because something else was working to ease the pressure off the labour market. That something was Gulf money.

It was in the 1980s that the interdependence between construction labour and agricultural labour discussed earlier became close. Construction had a peculiar significance. A great deal of the Gulf money went into private construction and, given the state's settlement pattern, a great deal of it was invested in dwellings next to the agricultural land and in the agricultural village. That proximity made construction wage a kind of reservation wage for other manual workers. This was the argument in the first major study that noticed the interdependence.[13] But that was not all. Construction workers were in high demand in the Gulf, and this profession was losing skilled artisans faster than other professions.[14] Therefore, construction drew in people from other local livelihoods, and yet the wage growth there did not slow until an inevitable slowdown in the construction boom itself.

The upshot was that, as the century ended, 'there is no peasant class in Kerala any longer'.[15] The trade unions had been so successful in the political field as to reduce their main constituent into a minor livelihood. In that process, their ally was migrant remittances that opened alternative forms of employment and sustained consumption even as agriculture declined steadily.

State income and employment data capture the story well enough for the 1990s and beyond. National and state income datasets include traditional and plantation agriculture together in measures of income and employment. This is potentially confusing because the former is in decline and the latter has been experiencing a resurgence since the 1990s. Further, the former is highly labour-intensive, but the latter is labour-intensive until the trees grow to maturity and not after. Subject to these cautions, the income share of the 'primary sector' fell from 33 per cent in 1993 to 10 per cent in 2017. In the first half of this timespan, the fall and the percentages were of a similar order as in India. In the second half, the proportion fell much faster in the state. The primary sector accounted for about 18–20 per cent of India's gross domestic product around 2020. A further divergence was in the employment share of

---

[13] Krishnan, 'Wages, Employment, and Output'.

[14] Mridul Eapen, 'Rural Non-Agricultural Employment in Kerala: Some Emerging Tendencies', *Economic and Political Weekly* 29, no. 21 (1994): 1285–96.

[15] Sukumaran Nair, 'Rural Labour Market', L-52.

the primary sector, which was significantly lower in the state to begin with. From 49 per cent in 1993, the share came down to about 32 in 2020; the corresponding percentages for India were 65 and 48. Considering the growth of side activity and non-farm businesses, the percentage is misleading. More people in the state combine activities than their counterparts elsewhere in India.

The primary sector is a combination of several disparate things: agriculture, livestock, fishing and mining, among others. If we take agriculture alone, the tendency for a relative fall stands, though the percentages become a bit shakier. Kerala would still stand out as a special case against the Indian average. However, a relative fall does not mean an absolute fall. Measured in cropped land, there was no sign of an absolute fall. There was a crisis in the 1970s and part of the 1980s, but cropped land held steady in the long run. The fall was acute in the most conventional crop, paddy. It was only here that all the elements of the dynamics previously discussed – labour intensity of operation, shortages, unionisation, and withdrawal of investment – were at work in full force.

The 1980s turnaround had happened partly because of a relative shift towards tree crops that generated higher growth and yield. Once that prospect was exhausted, agricultural output growth fell again in the 1990s and stayed low in the 2000s. In this context, a discourse on farm crisis returned. Those who had few options to combine agriculture with other jobs, or migrate away to better jobs, included many who belonged to the Dalits. The crisis discourse, therefore, also had a caste and tribe dimension. Among this set, the benefits of high wages had long worn off. Some had taken cheap farm loans and were unable to repay. A 1975 law to protect the interests of distressed farm workers and a welfare fund to help those in dire need were in operation, but their implementation was slowed by insufficient administrative capacity and obstructive moves by farmer lobbies.

The crisis had been complicated by the emergence of a credit market in the 1990s. A land mortgage is not a viable business almost anywhere in India because of a variety of legal and political restraints on transfers of title. Kerala was no exception. The loans were mostly unsecured. They were made after the government (federal with nationalised banks and state with cooperatives) insisted the bankers accommodate poor farmers.

Most of these loans (unlike in India) were not for investment in the farms. They were taken to finance the start of a business on the side or, occasionally, for consumption, marriage and working capital finance. About 11 per cent of the loans (according to a survey in 2007) was for farming. Those who took the loans were trying to meet the rising costs of cultivation, partly because the costs of new inputs like pesticides had risen.

A great deal of the loans was unpayable. Relatively small changes in prices drove many farmers to the wall. The government was not involved in deciding what happened when a farmer became bankrupt. The scenario, it turned out in the early 2000s, was explosive in many regions of India. Farmers facing bankruptcy committed suicide, ironically consuming the pesticides they had bought with borrowed money. The deaths were not small, isolated cases but happened in large numbers. Perhaps more than elsewhere, those who killed themselves had turned alcohol-dependent recently. In this way, caste, credit, crises and cravings for alcohol got entangled in a way that no state could possibly sort out easily.[16]

In the 2010s, farmer suicides caused much less worry to the state governments than before because generous credit write-offs had reduced its scale. The central message – agriculture did not pay at the current input costs – was not lost on the farmers who had the opportunity to take up a supplementary job.

Outside paddy, the scenario was mixed. There was continued modest output growth, almost no employment growth and, overall, while these activities did not actually retreat, they made a modest contribution at best to the average income, which grew at an exponential rate after 2000. Whether the activities survived or not, the drivers of income growth shifted out of agriculture and the primary sector decisively.

Plantations and Tree Crops

Even as paddy cultivation fell, there was growth in the cropped area, output and employment in rubber, coconut, fruits, orchard, spices and even tea. The trend had begun early but consolidated in the 1980s. The divergence between field crops and tree crops had grown sharply in the 1990s. By the end of the decade, most people took part in field crop cultivation as a subsidiary activity

---

[16] P. D. Jeromi, 'Farmers' Indebtedness and Suicides: Impact of Agricultural Trade Liberalisation in Kerala', *Economic and Political Weekly* 42, no. 31 (2007): 3241–47.

to something else that was their main income provider. Tree crops, on the other hand, provided more paying, steady and primary employment to more people.

Coconut was an exception. But in all other cases, and especially rubber, spices and tea, the natural advantage of the state was a geographical one. Climate and topography favoured their production in certain types of land that were not suitable for field crops. Already in the colonial and princely state era, foreign enterprise and their princely allies had exploited this advantage well enough (Chapter 2). This was nothing new, though, as Chapter 4 shows, the comparative advantage was lost in the postcolonial decades because of the retreat of foreign capital and restrictions on the export of agricultural goods.

The 1990s changed that. India's economic reforms meant not only a voluntary reduction of trade barriers but also compliance with the World Trade Organization's rules, which helped some parts of the heavily protected and sheltered agricultural sector to start exporting again. That turn was a very positive one for some of the tree crops. Now a new factor was added. Commercial agriculture of this type was less labour-intensive once the trees had grown to maturity. The high-wage syndrome in the state damaged field crops but left the tree crop sector relatively unscathed.[17]

Between 1970 and 2002, the proportion of cropped land under coffee, tea, rubber, coconut and spices doubled, most of the growth coming in the 1990s. These were not all similar. Coconut grew in small holdings, often adjacent to homesteads and agricultural land. The intensity of cultivation increased, and more fallows were converted into coconut lands. That was a long-term trend. Not much change happened in cashew and tea cultivation. The most impressive growth happened in spices, especially pepper, and in rubber. The growth had its downsides. The fortunes of all these crops depended on the condition of the world market and the emergence of competitors. Episodes of depressed prices lasting several years led to crises in rubber. In pepper, competitors emerged in Southeast Asia and South America. Still, these activities, by generating complementary industries like spice extracts and rubber products, played a role in the more recent business revival in the state.

---

[17] Brigit Joseph and K. J. Joseph, 'Commercial Agriculture in Kerala after the WTO', *South Asia Economic Journal* 6, no. 37 (2005): 37–57.

Women as Landowners and Agricultural Workers

The long-term pattern of change had specific implications for women workers. Both migration to take up jobs in distant places and diversification of livelihoods locally were male-biased processes. That is, more men than women took part in both. Comparatively more women were left in traditional fields like agriculture and plantations. But because agriculture was under pressure and many men had left active landholding and agricultural operations, the circumstances in which women worked changed, often quite radically.

One way the circumstances changed was to leave women as landowners and in charge of agricultural operations in some cases. Some even sold lands on their own. Tree crops were more women-friendly than field crops because the operations involved were different. Research done in the late 1990s explored what that extra responsibility meant in terms of authority and autonomy within the family and concluded that it did not mean much. Legally and socially, women's autonomy as property owners was limited by their role in the family.[18]

The exit of men and the alternatives available to them took the wind off the trade unions' sails. Wage negotiations were neither as vital nor as militant an activity as before. For the women, it was a harder struggle to negotiate wages. Access to finance was strongly gender-biased in this state as elsewhere. Since this study was done, the circumstances may have changed for the better, not least because of the emergence of a cooperative credit sector in the state. But the continued decline of traditional agriculture also reduced the scope for positive changes overall, for men or for women.

Conclusion

This is a story of a decline, brought on by global, India-wide and local factors. This story of a journey into irrelevance bears no repeating. Experts have mixed feelings about the journey. Influential scholars like K. P. Kannan think that the situation demands state intervention. By and large, economists register and analyse the decline but do not think it is reversible.

---

[18] Shoba Arun, 'Does Land Ownership Make a Difference? Women's Roles in Agriculture in Kerala, India', *Gender and Development* 7, no. 3 (1999): 19–27.

The aftermath of the agricultural decline had many dimensions. The insufficiency of food in the state led to a variety of adaptive strategies in policy. Kerala now produces less than 15 per cent of the foodgrains consumed in the state, so it relies heavily on the central pool to meet its rice and wheat requirements. Food security for all is a major policy goal, and public distribution of food plays a more critical political role than in other states. The state identified impoverished households, brought them under the rationing system and helped the local communities with food during the recent natural disasters (the Ockhi cyclone of 2017, the Nipah virus outbreak, floods in 2018 and 2019 and Covid-19). In keeping with the United Nations Sustainable Development Goals for 2030, the state has also initiated the Subhiksha Keralam programme, focusing on increasing food production by enhancing the area under cultivation and introducing advanced technologies for income and employment generation. The state has unique subsidy schemes to contain food inflation in the state.

There is a new perception that intervention in agriculture has a role to play in slowing environmental degradation in the state. From early in the twentieth century, expansion in cultivation and settlements led to a rapid loss of forest cover. The area under forests was estimated at 44 per cent of the total geographical area in 1905. It declined to 7–10 per cent in 1983. The loss of forests resulted in landslides and soil erosion, which had been accelerated by the introduction of crops such as tapioca in the hilly areas. Rainfall had been declining since the 1960s, making drought risk an additional cost for farming operations. The water control projects in the Kuttanad region led to the growth of aquatic weeds. Drainage systems broke down sometimes.

There was a case for protecting and reviving traditional agriculture. Rice cultivation was good at retaining soil nutrients. The growing demand for organic food had imparted a modest kind of impetus for traditional rainfed agriculture. The prospect of a food crisis is forever present in a state that never produced enough for its population and now produces a lot less. These concerns have not yet translated into a major new policy initiative.

A rather similar story repeats with private enterprise until 1990, when a revival began. The next chapter describes the fall and rise.

4

Capital

Retreat and Resurgence

When India became independent, the main livelihoods in this region, as in the rest of the country, were based on land. But unlike most other regions of India, a significant and relatively more prominent part of the economy (half or more of the domestic product) was urban and non-agricultural. Non-agricultural did not mean industrial. True, the processing of some commercial products involved non-mechanised factories. Alappuzha (Alleppey) had emerged as a hub of coir production and Quilon (Kollam) of cashew. Some isolated large, mechanised factories employed hundreds of people in one place in chemicals, rayon, paper and a few other lines. Thus, Aluva (Alwaye) had textiles, fertilisers, aluminium, glass and rayon industries, and Ernakulam oil and soap industries. There were also tea estates in the hills. A concentration of plantation businesses in rubber and spices occurred to the east of Kottayam. But collectively, these formed a smaller group than trade and the financing of marketing, which dominated the landscape of non-agricultural employment. All major towns lived mainly on trade and informal banking. Trichur and Kottayam were mostly service-based towns, with a concentration of banks, colleges and rich churches.

Over one-third of the workforce was in industry, trade, commerce and finance. In most large states of India, the percentage was 20–35.[1] The exceptions were the industrialised states of West Bengal and Maharashtra, where factory-based large-scale industrial firms concentrated. Again, a contrast emerged with the rest of India. Most local businesses were small-scale, semi-rural and household enterprises, whereas non-agricultural enterprises in the rest of India were mainly urban.

---

[1] Government of India, *Census of India, 1951: Travancore-Cochin* (New Delhi: Government of India, 1953).

Further, industrialisation almost everywhere else signified a sharp inequality between the countryside and the city. The former was trapped in low-yield farmland producing grains for subsistence or local markets, and the latter experienced growth of high-wage jobs. In the state, that distance was narrower. The presence of tree crops and their industrial processing made for a narrower gap between the rural and the urban. Many of the landholders were also owners of estates growing tree crops. Agriculture was not necessarily low yield nor subsistence oriented. In this way, agriculture and non-agriculture, rural and urban came much closer here compared with India.

Then came a fall. Although the chapter will sometimes call the phenomenon 'de-industrialisation', the primary process was not just the loss of industry but the loss of synergy between industry, banking and commerce, which synergy was the backbone of the regional economic system. 'De-commercialisation' or de-capitalisation would be just as appropriate a term for this retreat. At its roots, there was a retreat of private capital from both industrial production and trading.

The Retreat of Private Capital

'In 1950, the per capita manufacturing product of Travancore of Rs. 48 was significantly higher than the all-India figure of Rs. 37.'[2] Thirty years after the formation of the state, 'Kerala is an industrially backward state'.[3] Ten years later, 'Kerala is [still] one of the least industrially developed states of the union'.[4] It is remarkable how laid-back experts were about asking why this fall happened and if it was inevitable. So far, there is little systematic historical research on how a semi-industrial region could lose its lead in manufacturing and even de-industrialise between 1956 and 1990. What happened?

After independence, the Government of India repressed old-style foreign capital. Restrictions on the managing agency contract, employment of

---

[2] C. T. Kurien, 'Kerala's Development Experience: Random Comments about the Past and Some Considerations for the Future', *Social Scientist* 23, nos. 1–3 (1995): 50–69, 55.

[3] P. M. Mathew, 'Exploitation of Women Labour: An Analysis of Women's Employment in Kerala', *Social Scientist* 13, nos. 10–11 (1985): 28–47, 29.

[4] Sunil Mani, 'Economic Liberalisation and Kerala's Industrial Sector: An Assessment of Investment Opportunities', *Economic and Political Weekly* 31, no. 34 (1996): 2323–30, 2323.

personnel from abroad, overvalued exchange, and a virtual blockade upon foreign remittance and import of machines from abroad led to an almost across-the-board decline in the tea companies and an abrupt withdrawal from exports. The governments of Kerala and Tamil Nadu did not want to fall behind in this race to the bottom. Land ceiling legislation and a high rate of agricultural income tax targeted foreign firms and significantly reduced their capacity to make investments.

Most European-owned trading firms left the state, leading to undercapitalisation of trading and plantations and damaging overseas business ties. The tea plantations industry did not exactly decline but did need to reorient from export to the domestic market, which damaged the market for higher-quality orthodox tea.

Other industries gave little cause for cheer. Both coir rope making and cashew nut processing were very labour-intensive and employed many women from rural households. These industries existed because the raw material, raw nut and coconut fibre, were available in plenty in the state. In the 1960s and 1970s, this employment started to shift away from factories to households and small workshops to escape minimum wage legislation and regulation by the factory acts. Because the enforcement of these regulations was state-based, the business could quickly relocate to neighbouring Tamil Nadu.[5] In other words, there was no decline in cashew, only a massive capital flight.

With abundant coconut trees, Kerala had a natural advantage in producing coir yarn, rope and mat. The demand was worldwide. Until 1950, the primary market for coir products was abroad. A string of British and American trading firms organised the marketing. The manufacturing process was semi-manual, and attempts to install power looms failed. The industry was organised in large factories, hiring several hundred workers at a time and employing them at piece rates. Some of these factories were foreign-owned, but most were not.[6]

The industry faced a modest shock in the 1930s when a strong trade union movement emerged, and the state failed to intervene in the industrial disputes

---

[5] K. P. Kannan, 'Employment, Wages, and Conditions of Work in the Cashew Processing Industry', working paper of Centre for Development Studies (Trivandrum), 1978.

[6] T. M. Thomas Isaac, 'Class Struggle and Structural Changes: Coir Mat and Matting Industry in Kerala, 1950–80', *Economic and Political Weekly* 17, no. 31 (1982): PE13–PE29.

that followed. A much bigger shock unfolded shortly after independence. Foreign firms retracted their investment and eventually left the industry just when substitutes for rope and mats were beginning to become popular. The exit reduced market access of the manufacturers since the most prominent trading firms to leave were foreign-owned. Standard histories of the period treat this exit with remarkable nonchalance, as if it were in the fitness of things that an independent country should kick out foreign capitalists. The dislike for foreign investment of the past stands in peculiar contrast to the hankering after foreign investment in the present. The exit of foreign capital was not inevitable and left a negative legacy.

In coir, the de-capitalisation and de-industrialisation were long-drawn processes. In the 1950s, the trade union movement flared up again because many manufacturers felt retrenchment was inevitable. Raising productivity was beyond the competence of the domestic employers, and they could cut production and wages instead. When the negotiations failed, the employers of the large factories started contracting with small-scale manufacturing establishments that were outside the scope of regulation. The market for coir stabilised with the growth of the domestic market. But the large-scale production system developed on the back of the export market collapsed.

In the 1960s and 1970s, the state government nationalised some ailing industrial firms. Together with the state enterprises started by the Travancore government or later, these formed a substantial basket of state-owned enterprises. With few exceptions, if any, public-sector firms made losses. A survey done in 1990 found two reasons why these performed poorly. They were highly leveraged, and debt was costly. And partly due to indifferent management and partly due to a shortage of money, the firms neglected the modernisation of their technological setup.[7]

A study done in 1990 of the entire corporate sector in the state again came to a negative conclusion. 'The industrial performance of Kerala,' the paper said, 'is relatively poor. This fact is reflected in almost every relevant indicator.'[8] Analysing the performance, the paper identified one overriding factor in many companies, over-reliance on high-cost debt capital.

---

[7] P. Mohanan Pillai, 'Whither State Sector Enterprises in Kerala?' *Economic and Political Weekly* 25, nos. 7/8 (1990): M9–M16.

[8] Nirmala Padmanabhan, 'Poor Performance of Private Corporate Sector in Kerala', *Economic and Political Weekly* 25, no. 37 (1990): 2071–75, 2071.

In contemporary discourses, it was often said that managerial failures were a matter of outlook and drive and could be resolved with workers' participation in management. The idea had a lot of traction in socialist-leaning circles. The state saw at least one case of large-scale transfer of managerial authority from private owners to workers (Tata Finlay Tea). Still, where this idea was tried, it 'has produced only limited results'.[9] The lack of democratisation was not the problem. Debt dependence and lack of modernisation were the problems, and both syndromes owed to one thing, de-capitalisation. Workers managing or even owning a company are not often credible borrowers because their expertise is restricted to the shopfloor alone. De-capitalisation joined the traditional industries, plantations, the corporate sector and public firms in one single story.

In a nutshell, Kerala, with a relatively larger industrial economy at independence, lost its lead. It did not because relative factor prices changed, but the supply of private capital withdrew. Why?

De-industrialisation: Theories

Discussions on industrial and business trends were distinctly pessimistic until the 1990s, even as excitement about the 'Kerala Model' grew. In the quarter century after the formation of the state, the average growth rate of employment in the manufacturing industry was below the average for India and most southern states.[10] These were the years when the public sector in the states and at the federal level was expanding to stimulate industrial production and diversification. Kerala was no exception to that trend. But the result was unimpressive.

Interpretations of the development of non-agricultural enterprises in the state focused on why the state did not industrialise more. No answer to a question about something that did not happen can ever be verified. But the question did encourage more research on the problems of the industries that did happen.

One strand in this scholarship said that an aggressive trade union movement scared away prospective investors. The argument was relevant in

---

[9] Mohanan Pillai, 'Whither State Sector Enterprises'.

[10] Alice Albin, 'Manufacturing Sector in Kerala: Comparative Study of Its Growth and Structure', *Economic and Political Weekly* 25, no. 37 (1990): 2059–70.

traditional industries like tea, cashew and coir. Studying small industries on both sides of the Kerala–Tamil Nadu border, often under the ownership of people from the former state, M. A. Oommen concluded that the trade union movement had led to a flight of capital from the state.[11] A careful re-examination of the evidence does find that Kerala in the 1970s and 1980s had an above-average incidence of industrial disputes and a vast number of person-days lost, showing the capacity for disputes to last a long time. The figures, when compared with the relatively low industrial base of the state, were staggering.[12] In the 1990s, person-days lost fell significantly, but by then the perception that the state was a high-wage place not safe to do business in had become entrenched, a sample survey of prospective investors found.[13]

Another opinion was that the way industries developed in the long run was too fragmented, with little synergy between one enterprise and another.[14] Specifically, the major forms of factory in the late twentieth century – chemicals, rubber and tobacco products – were like autonomous islands. Few large factories produced a significant legacy of 'downstream' industries using the main products coming from these.[15] That may be right, but more is needed to explain why these companies should run losses consistently. With or without linkage effects, most companies and the corporate industrial sector posted a dreadfully bad record between 1970 and 1990.

In a public lecture reflecting on the state's development experience, the economist C. T. Kurien said that the princely state economies had sponsored one kind of market integration based on export commodities. In contrast, post-independence India saw another type, based on domestic food trade and fiscal transfers for industrialisation.[16] This is true, but the causes of the retreat from exports are unsaid. The observation does not pursue enough the impact

[11] M. A. Oommen, 'Mobility of Small Scale Entrepreneurs: A Kerala Experience', *Indian Journal of Industrial Relations* 17, no. 1 (1981): 65–87.
[12] M. M. Thampy, 'Wage-Cost and Kerala's Industrial Stagnation: Study of Organised Small-Scale Sector', *Economic and Political Weekly* 25, no. 37 (1990): 2077–82.
[13] Mani, 'Economic Liberalisation and Kerala's Industrial Sector'.
[14] K. K. Subrahmanian and P. Mohanan Pillai, 'Kerala's Industrial Backwardness: Exploration of Alternative Hypotheses', *Economic and Political Weekly* 21, no. 14 (1986): 577–92.
[15] Jayan Jose Thomas, 'Kerala's Industrial Backwardness: A Case of Path Dependence in Industrialization?' *World Development* 33, no. 5 (2005): 763–83.
[16] C. T. Kurien, 'Kerala's Development Experience: Random Comments about the Past and Some Considerations for the Future', *Social Scientist* 23, nos. 1–3 (1995): 50–69.

of a withdrawal from global commerce, nor says why that withdrawal was necessary or inevitable.

A further argument, primarily from the radical left, was that the drain of internal financial resources to outside the state compromised local investment. The drain occurred at two levels: through the stock exchanges, particularly after the opening of the Cochin Stock Exchange in 1978, and through commercial and nationalised banks. The middle class with their savings purchased stocks of companies operating outside the state. Banks in the state maintained a relatively low credit-to-deposit ratio. There is some indication that the ratio has remained low even in recent years.[17] Again, this phenomenon would not explain why domestic industry did badly, and may have been a response to the de-industrialisation.

Others have attributed the de-industrialisation to a Dutch disease process. A Dutch disease syndrome refers to the concentration of resources in one sector promising high returns at the expense of the wider economy. In this case, the Gulf migration boom drew savings and investment away from traditional fields towards consumption or construction. That process did occur. But the decline had older roots. It was well on its way before Gulf remittances became a serious flow.[18]

Most of these assessments about the decline lack historical sense. To explain the post-independence de-industrialisation, it is necessary first to understand the causes of colonial-era industrialisation. This is rarely done, and the scholars who engage with the decline do not engage enough with the reasons for the colonial pattern of industrial development.

The reason was that, whereas the colonial development pattern was market-led, that is, it utilised the state's comparative advantage in natural resources and labour, the postcolonial one was not. The range of resources available for commercial use was enormous and greater than most other states in India. If the region lacked the capital to invest, the princely states were wise enough to permit the flow of foreign investment with little barrier to meet that gap. The decline happened because the state neglected to rely on these comparative advantages. Indian big business by and large did not

---

[17] K. T. Rammohan and K. Ravi Raman, 'Of Cochin Stock Exchange and What It Means?' *Economic and Political Weekly* 25, no. 1 (1990): 17–19.

[18] K. N. Harilal and K. J. Joseph, 'Stagnation and Revival of Kerala Economy. An Open Economy Perspective', working paper of Centre for development Studies (Trivandrum), 2000.

understand the export trade in spices or tea and were not attracted by the opportunities in the state as foreign capital left. There was nothing inevitable about this fall. It resulted from bad choices by the states in independent India in charge of generating economic growth.

The Fall Illustrated

Travancore's industrial lead (and Cochin's and, to a lesser extent, Malabar's) had owed to global connections. The export of commodities like coir, cashew, spices, timber, rubber, tea and coffee sustained it. Global trading firms organised the overseas export side. These goods needed processing in factories and, in turn, stimulated plantations, banking and commercial services where indigenous capitalists like the Syrian Christians played a significant role.

The first bad choice was to discriminate against and neglect export-oriented traditional industries (more on this later). There was never a policy after independence to sustain the dynamism in these sectors, which would need nurturing the global links on which these were based. Instead, tax, remittance and exchange rates were so manipulated as to drive foreign capital out of these businesses. The industries faced a fall in exports and a forced reorientation towards the domestic market (in tea, coir) that took only the poorer quality products.

With their financial capacity impaired, the employers in these businesses tried to squeeze workers and soon ran into trouble with them. Where they could, these traditional industries fled their homes to go to Tamil Nadu, where wages were lower and labour was less unionised. That was not all. Women, particularly from the socially oppressed castes, worked in large numbers in traditional industries, so the decline badly affected women's paid work opportunities. A handloom weaving industry had developed in Cannanore (Kannur) district. Since the 1970s, the industry had started to shift operations to Tamil Nadu, mainly in response to the lower wages of women workers there.

A second bad choice was to promote big factories in a socialistic style with taxpayer money. These were little islands with few connections and little positive legacies. In the 1970s and 1980s, most public-sector factories struggled to raise capital, became dependent on high-cost debts and went quietly bankrupt.

After 1956, European trading firms steadily exited spice exports. While a central government entity called the Spices Board took some part in marketing the product, it was poor compensation, and the business was subdued because its marketing was undercapitalised. A good example is the valuable cash crop, black pepper. Once a major export, the marketing system suffered the exit of private trading firms. In the first twenty–twenty-five years after the formation of the state, the production, export and productivity of black pepper either did not change or changed for the worse. Meanwhile, the main area growing the crop shifted from the northern and central highlands to the south. The shift was probably a reaction to a pest attack, which was beyond the capability of the new marketing system to address. Whereas once private traders would gather and dispense knowledge, knowledge now 'came under the purview of multiple actors under the Spices Board, Ministry of Commerce, Government of India and State Government. However, there is very limited coordination between different agencies involved in the promotion of this crop'.[19]

The more traditional plantations in the state could have fared better. A strongly unionised workforce and rising wages squeezed profits in this labour-intensive industry. One of the largest tea producers in south India, the Kannan Devan Hills Plantations, was an affiliate of the James Finlay group. The Tata Group purchased it in 1976 and gave up control in 2005. Another struggling survivor was Malankara Plantations, started in 1910 by P. John and mainly engaged in rubber and coconut. The company did well before independence and continued to expand in the three decades after independence. The 1980s were the years of crisis when industrial disputes led to the near-closure of factories. In the 1990s, it lost considerable estate land to the government due to land reforms.

Spices and rubber persisted as significant fields of investment among Indian groups, especially the Syrian Christians. Several Christian farmers migrated from the Kottayam district plains to the Idukki uplands in the last decade of Travancore's rule. Food shortages induced migration after World War II, and the government encouraged it. These farms started to

---

[19] A. Sajitha, 'Regional Variations in the Performance of Black Pepper Cultivation in Kerala: An Exploration of Non Price Factors', paper for National Research Programme on Plantation Development, Centre for Development Studies, Trivandrum, 2014, 50.

grow spices, mainly cardamom. The hills were known to be suitable for spice growing, as a few British planters had shown in the nineteenth century.

Rubber plantations began as export-oriented plantation businesses like tea and coffee in the late nineteenth century. Not being especially capital-intensive, it attracted considerable indigenous capital. At independence, British interest in rubber was relatively smaller than the Indian interest but not marginal. The Great Depression, however, had hit exports hard, and the post-independence revival of the industry, particularly after the reorganisation of the Rubber Board in 1954, saw the exit of export-oriented firms and foreign capital, and the growth of firms serving the domestic demand for rubber.[20]

In the 1990s, economists lamented the failure of industrialisation. Still, macroeconomic data pointed in another direction.

The Transition Moment

Average growth rates of domestic product in the state, around 1 per cent in 1961–75, fell to near-zero in 1975–85. But this was not a decline across the board. The tertiary sector or services such as trade, transport, finance and hospitality did very well. The primary sector (crop production, fishery) showed little sign of life, except for livestock. The secondary sector, including manufacturing, also posted little growth.[21] Employment did grow in manufacturing. But the average trend comprised two parts: traditional industries such as cashew and coir, and modern industries such as chemicals and aluminium. The former lost many jobs, whereas the latter, fed with public money, created jobs.

Around 1987, agriculture had become an insignificant employer, with hardly 16 per cent of the workforce engaged in it, and the proportion came down to nearly 10 per cent in 2020. The decline in agricultural employment happened for an obvious reason: the ratio of wages earned in the growth

---

[20] K. Tharian George, V. Haridasan and B. Sreekumar, 'Role of Government and Structural Changes in Rubber Plantation Industry', *Economic and Political Weekly* 23, no. 48 (1988): M158–M166.

[21] K. P. Kannan, 'Kerala Economy at the Crossroads?' *Economic and Political Weekly* 25, nos. 35–36 (1990): 1951–56.

sectors to that in farming was above one and rising.[22] It did not make sense for ordinary people to be farming land for wages.

From the 1990s, a second phase in the transition had begun, partly driven by Gulf money. Employment grew significantly in plantations, construction and retail trade, especially consumer goods and construction materials. Almost all these sectors had gained from the Gulf remittances. These recapitalised plantations modestly, stimulating consumption, residential construction and trade. Per-head consumption levels exceeded the Indian average significantly at the end of the 1980s. A 1996 study found that rather than new investment, a significant improvement in capacity utilisation in some consumer goods contributed to the revival in growth.[23]

In these transition years, the Malayalam film industry flourished. Gulf money flowed into cinema and cinema halls. The number of theatres increased. The number of productions increased substantially. The quality of films became very diverse. Creative, experimental and art cinema produced some of their best works in the 1980s. At another end, undeclared incomes were invested in cheap and shoddy productions, sometimes bordering on the obscene. A thread running through this odd combination was the intent to gauge the new consumerist culture of the small towns. Cinemagoers lost interest in the poorer-quality products soon enough. The advent of television in the late 1980s and a huge number of dud films led to a crisis in the industry. Partly because of almost continuous financial pressure, the Malayalam industry stayed artisanal rather than concentrating in mega studios, as the business did in Tamil Nadu, Hyderabad and Mumbai.

A third phase in the transition unfolded around 2000. We will use one word – capitalism – to suggest what has been driving the change in recent decades. The term captures large-scale deployment of capital, expansion of old family businesses, entry into new fields that required significant technological advancement, and withdrawal of the state as a direct investor in business assets. These processes are always risky because long-term capital is relatively scarce and high cost in any state in India. Access to capital (and markets) abroad built during the Gulf boom came in handy to mitigate that problem. In that limited sense, there was a return to the princely state heritage of integration with the world economy.

---

[22] Mridul Eapen, 'Rural Non-Agricultural Employment in Kerala: Some Emerging Tendencies', *Economic and Political Weekly* 29, no. 21 (1994): 1285–96.

[23] Mani, 'Economic Liberalisation and Kerala's Industrial Sector'.

The Resurgence of Capitalism since 2000

After 2000, and especially after 2010, the average real domestic product in the state has grown faster than the Indian average for most years and significantly above the near-zero rates that prevailed in the 1970s and 1980s. This time, the secondary sector had revived and joined the services sector. The average growth rate for the 2010s was 5–7 per cent per year in both industry and services (see also Chapter 6). That change was no longer driven by remittance-fuelled consumption. New forms of business investment led it. The third phase in the turnaround had owed to India's economic liberalisation that had just begun. The tariff reforms, partial retraction of regulation and state enterprise, and easier rules for foreign investment stimulated investment in export-oriented businesses, both the old kind (natural-resource-intensive) and the new kind (information technology or skill-intensive).

The last quarter century changed the business scene completely. A string of medium- and large-scale companies emerged in manufacturing and services. Almost all started as small family businesses. Some remained family enterprises throughout; others inducted non-family management early. The fields that saw the most growth included some traditional ones like spices and gold, but with significant changes in the products offered. However, most fields were relatively new and knowledge-intensive, if not capital-intensive. The profile of the people who set these up shows why they began here.

Although the government did not directly stimulate this revival, it did indirectly help, most visibly in leading a much-hyped and overrated drive to encourage tourism in the state.

Selling Nature

Kerala has always attracted tourists thanks to its extraordinary natural beauty. A long coastline, mountains, forests and backwaters offer tourists a whole package of experiences. But as a business, tourism and hotels were underdeveloped until 1980. The Persian Gulf money changed that to some extent. New hotels were built in the 1980s. That and local investment went into infrastructure for tourism in several places. It was still an uncoordinated effort.

In the 1990s, the government stepped in. Hoping to utilise the private sector's lead in investment, it announced a desire to develop destinations in partnership with private parties. The parties were diverse, including local entrepreneurs interested in setting up homestays and established hotel chains like Oberoi and Taj.

In 2000, some collaborating groups launched an advertising campaign with the catchy slogan, 'Kerala: God's own country'.[24] By then, it was clear that the state saw tourism as a 'development option'.[25] In the next decade, the government spent a lot of money advertising in European languages to capture a bigger share of foreign tourists. How successful the hype about being god's own country was can be debated. While international tourist flow did grow in the state following these initial efforts, it did not develop any faster than tourism in India. Even now, the state is the eighth or ninth among Indian states receiving foreign tourists. However, its ranking is higher as a destination for domestic tourists. About 90 per cent of the tourist inflow were Indians, untouched by the god's own country advertisements printed in German or French newspapers.

Indian tourists responded to the growth of tourism infrastructure in the state rather than any advertisement. There was a reason why it did. Quality and cleanliness are sold at a considerable premium in the Indian hotel industry. The business of hotels grew in the recent decades with rising middle-class living standards but did not mature enough to deliver international quality for a reasonable price. Most Indian hotels employed men for housekeeping, unlike the rest of the world, where this service was managed by women, who have a better sense of cleanliness. For the price paid in, say, Pune or Nagpur or Allahabad, a hotel room in Kochi (Cochin) was likely to be more decent, and the food served better and safer. These essential quality markers mattered to domestic tourists. Besides, as mentioned before, Kerala was not one place but a package of diverse experiences.

The campaign did deliver unique value. Offbeat and experimental ventures forged ahead along with conventional hotels. The offbeat lines were sustainable tourism, 'experience' tourism, where tourists experience history by staying in a recreated Jewish merchant home in Kochi, for example, and

[24] Ganga Dhanesh, 'Kerala. *God's Own Country*: From Backwaters to One of the Ten Paradises on Earth', in *Public Relations Cases: International Perspectives*, ed. Danny Moss, Melanie Powell, Barbara DeSanto, 40–58 (Abingdon: Routledge, 2010).
[25] T. T. Sreekumar and Govindan Parayil, 'Contentions and Contradictions of Tourism as Development Option: The Case of Kerala, India', *Third World Quarterly* 23, no. 3 (2002): 529–48.

health tourism, when tourists combine sightseeing with yoga classes and Ayurveda treatments. Among many who pioneered these enterprises, Jose Dominic, a hotelier in Lakshadweep, is especially well known.[26] A much larger flow of money went into the more conventional forms of investment: hotels, resorts, boutiques and retail malls.

After hotels, the industry most closely associated with tourism was Ayurvedic therapy. The Travancore princes sponsored the first Ayurveda College in 1889. In 1902, a private treatment centre came up in Kottakkal in the north, now a heritage business. The initial success of Arya Vaidya Sala of Kottakkal had owed to its founder P. S. Varier's (1869–1944) decision to mass produce and package medicines and standardise formulas, an unheard-of concept in Ayurvedic treatment, which was patient-specific, with the drugs precisely customised. In the hands of his grandson, clinical research expanded, aimed at incorporating scientific practices in particular fields where Ayurveda had strength. Since 1900, the teaching of the subject has spread to other towns in the south of the state. Although the state was home to many natural plants used in Ayurvedic treatment, the sale of herbal medicine and health products did not develop much until 1990. After that, the market exploded.

After 2000, Ayurveda network became closely connected with health tourism and tourism at large, strengthening both. Treatment courses and the production of herbal cures developed in parallel in the state. The Arya Vaidya Sala remains the market leader in treatment courses, with over 60 million dollars in revenue in 2022.

Outside hospitality and tourism, business at large revived in the 2000s due to several factors. Foreign investment flowed into the information technology (IT) industry around Thiruvananthapuram (Trivandrum) city, thanks to its better infrastructure and generally good quality of life compared with most Indian towns of mid-size. Around Ernakulam and northwards, industries and trading firms began to grow using natural resources such as spice, marine products, herbs, wood and rubber. Some of these were old firms that benefited from India's reintegration into the world economy. The fact that some were already exporting to the Gulf was an advantage.

Whereas the former pathway was completely new, the latter was consistent with the business development trajectory in the princely states and

---

[26] https://www.theweekendleader.com/Success/3136/street-smart.html (accessed 2 February 2024).

Malabar. Except that, almost all major firms processing or selling natural resources also invested in technology to diversify product range, manufacture products suited to industrial needs, or package better. Since 2000, a few old family business groups have re-emerged, partly through investment in marketing and export of the core business product and partly by diversifying out of it.

Old Groups Diversifying

An interesting case is Abad Fisheries. Usman Mohammed Hashim, a Kuchchhi businessman who moved to Kochi, started a marine product export business directed at the Burma (present-day Myanmar) market in 1932. The industry suffered during World War II but survived. After independence, it continued to sell canned goods and frozen seafood to European and North American markets. The economic reforms of the 1980s and 1990s helped exports grow. With eleven factories, four cold storages and 6 million dollars in revenue, the business is one of the largest of its kind in India now. Meanwhile, Abad had diversified into hotels, which emerged as one of its main earners in recent years. As domestic tourism grew, Abad was well placed with several hotels and resorts in key destinations.[27]

Industries like these long-surviving diversified family firms are rare. A few can still be found in rubber products, spice exports and plywood. Several are Syrian Christian enterprises. K. L. Francis, a coconut products trader in Irinjalakuda, Thrissur, was one such firm. In the 1990s, he began manufacturing coconut oil. The brand called Nirmal was reportedly the most popular in south India. In the 2000s, the oil extraction business sold its products in West Asia. The turnover of the company is well above 50 million dollars in 2020. Another coconut product firm, Kerala Solvent Extractions, began in the 1960s to process by-products of oil, which were used as cattle feed. It was well placed to exploit the recent shift to organic feed. The revenues are 50–60 million dollars.

Another conventional firm with an unconventional history was Vijaylaxmi Cashews, which started in the 1950s. K. Ravindranathan Nair hailed from a wealthy Kollam family. A part of his profits from the cashew

---

[27] Company website, and https://www.onmanorama.com/travel/kerala/2021/12/07/abad-group-hotels-riaz-ahmed.html (accessed 2 February 2024).

trading business was invested in film production, his lifelong passion. The business evolved into the leading cashew exporting firm (revenue in 2017 was 80 million dollars), mainly under the management of the next generation in the family.

Then a cluster of old and new companies engaged in spice trading and extraction. The spice trade revived in the 1980s. It began with cardamom production in the highlands. A new local variety was developed around 1987. And about fifteen–twenty-five years later, online and direct marketing began to develop. For the first time in history, relatively small plantation estates in the highlands could market their products directly, a system that is now quite common. From the 1990s, new and old enterprises strengthened the turnaround by investing in downstream products.

Old Fields Modernising

Akay Natural Ingredients was established in 1995. Alex Koshy, who started it, was an engineer in the United Arab Emirates. When the company was acquired by Oterra (2022), initially a joint venture with Akay and later a Danish company producing natural foods, Akay was a leading nutraceutical producer (natural foods with health benefits), with a 28-million-dollar turnover in 2022.

C. V. Jacob started as a cardamom trader in the 1950s. He later diversified into engineering contracts but returned to spice extracts. Synthite, begun in 1972, is a significant producer of spice extracts. In the 2000s, Synthite expanded into many related fields and became a conglomerate. It also moved into tourism and hotels. One of the new ventures was branded packaged spices traded by Intergrow Food and Beverages. The group turnover was around 400 million dollars in 2020. Also in spice extraction, Mane Kancor, by contrast, is a 1990s enterprise started by Geemon Korah, an agricultural scientist. Plant Lipids, a Kochi-based firm, started in the business of spice extracts in the late 1970s but expanded significantly in the 2000s. Its global presence increased, and its product range diversified into various materials outside Kerala. The group had a revenue of around 60–70 million dollars in 2020.

Among the more recent entrants, Arjuna Natural Extracts started in the early 2000s as a collaboration between a newspaper vendor and his brother-in-law, a biochemist, as a spice extract export company. It is one of the largest manufacturers of omega-3 fatty acids from fish oil in Asia and of turmeric extract. The founder P. J. Kunjachan figured as an example of an entrepreneur in business schools in India. The revenues stood at 50 million dollars in 2023.

Other significant examples of natural-resource-using firms would include Active Char, an activated carbon manufacturer using coconut shells, available in abundance in the state. Active carbon has uses in water filters and agriculture. The company had a revenue of 8 million dollars in 2022. The Mfar group that set it up in 2005 was headed by P. Mohamed Ali, known for one of the largest Indian-owned engineering firms in Oman, called Galfar. Ali hails from Thrissur. A second example is Sterling Farm Research, which started as a professional-run company making fertilisers. It later developed neopeat, a soil substitute made from coir. The coir pith is expected to find a growing market among private garden owners in Britain, which bans peat moss as a soil substitute.

Orthodox tea production in the highlands persists, if on a much lower key than in the colonial era. In 2005, Kannan Devan's 12,500 employees jointly purchased the company's shares. Since this changeover, the company has done well. But its good performances depended on the windfall of tea prices. In 2020, it posted sales of about 60 million dollars. A private Indian group fared better. Almost as large as Kannan Devan in employment and scale, AVT began in 1925, when Alfred Vedam Thomas bought pastureland in Pasuparai, Tamil Nadu, to grow tea. The AVT group later diversified from tea to other natural products, extracts and tissue cultures. Most of these diversifications happened in the 2000s. The group sales revenue was around 72 million dollars in 2022.

Although large-scale tea plantations could have done better, the Indian-owned rubber estates stimulated two relatively new downstream businesses: wood products and medical supplies. The processing of raw materials from rubber flourished in the state. One of these firms, Rubfila, a latex products maker, began in the 1990s. In 2022, its turnover stood at 50–55 million dollars. The industry also received foreign investment. The Texas rubber products maker Core invested in forming Vajra Rubber in Kerala, which exports almost all of its production of mainly automotive components.

The state was never a hub of small-scale textile production for export. Nothing like the small industry clusters one can see in Maharashtra, Tamil Nadu and areas around Delhi ever developed in the state. However, a textile industry did exist in the state before the economic reforms. Weaving skills were available, and the availability of bamboo pulp in plenty had encouraged the establishment of rayon plants. This business existed as a few isolated factories. Among them, the emergence of Kitex was meteoric.

Kochi-based Kitex Garments was set up in 1992 by M. C. Jacob. It is a world-leading manufacturer of infant wear, mainly catering to Asian markets, and has a turnover of over 100 million dollars. Jacob was a public works contractor who tried his hand at soap-making, trading in areca nuts and manufacturing aluminium and related products. The family business grew based on aluminium products, the spice trade and textiles. The group's other venture, producing aluminium utensils for the kitchen, continues to be a strong retail brand. Jacob's sons head separate companies.[28]

Like textiles, timber was an old industry in the state. In the nineteenth century, timber extraction and processing were major livelihoods in Malabar and Cochin. With restrictions on the felling of forest trees, logging and timber processing declined. Around 2000, restrictions on logging in forest areas had reduced the extent of the industry in Assam, the leader in plywood earlier.[29] It fell in the state too. But there was a twist to the story. Kerala had an abundant supply of rubber wood, a near-monopoly. Rubber wood is a hard wood suitable for a variety of uses. Sometimes rubber wood veneers can also be used in plywood. More generally, plywood is made of a range of woods not normally suited for other uses. As a construction boom began, first in the wake of the Gulf migration and later stimulated by the resurgence of economic growth and living standards, the plywood industry grew rapidly. Around Perumbavoor in Ernakulam district, a cluster of several hundred plywood factories were set up in the 2000s. A few of these factories were large enough to deserve space in business magazines and newspapers. The scale of the expansion was big enough to draw in hundreds of migrant workers from Assam, West Bengal, Odisha and Bihar.

Gold ornaments are the final example of a conventional line of business that revived to an extraordinary degree. Thrissur was associated with gold jewellery making and trading for over a hundred years. Between 1968 and 1990, the government of India restricted gold imports to conserve foreign

---

[28] https://www.forbesindia.com/article/family-business/sabu-and-bobby-jacob-cut-from-a-different-cloth/62983/1 (accessed 2 February 2024).

[29] Benoy Peter, 'Labour Migration to Kerala: The Case of Plywood Industry' (PhD dissertation of International Institute for Population Sciences, Mumbai, 2010).

exchange. Gold ornaments remained subdued during these years, and many ornaments were made by neighbourhood artisans rather than in large showrooms, which were rare. Thrissur, however, suffered less from the restrictive trade regime, thanks to a captive non-resident market in the Gulf and a large domestic market for gold ornaments.

The business grew fast with the repeal of the Gold Control Order of 1968. Several Thrissur firms invested in showrooms and retail marketing. With the growth of Kalyan Jewellers, perhaps the most famous of Thrissur firms, the retail business of some Thrissur companies expanded throughout India. Kalyan Jewellers had an annual revenue of over a billion dollars in 2022. As wages rose in the state, artisans from other states developed contracts with the jeweller firms, and many sent workers to the town to perform contracts. It is believed that nearly 200, 000 people lived directly or indirectly on gold in the town on the eve of the pandemic. The number of those from West Bengal and Rajasthan working in the industry remains fuzzy but should be in the thousands.

Since 1990, gold prices have been unstable in the international market. But in India, with an enormous domestic demand for jewellery, retail and design range expansion, and a rapid rise in middle-class living standards, prices have risen steadily since 1990. A particularly sharp increase occurred between 2003 and 2013. While inflation in gold is bad news for the jewellers' business, it is good news for another business that utilised the Indian consumers' desire for gold, that of gold-mortgaged loans. Such activity was not confined to this area. But the leader in this field, Muthoot Finance, is based in Kochi and has been expanding its turnover greatly since the early 2000s.

Muthoot Finance evolved from a trading firm set up in the 1880s, which diversified into gold loans at the end of the 1930s. The family had a timber trade business in the nineteenth century, which suffered losses during a flood in 1882, but recovered later. More diversifications happened in the twentieth century. However, the one into gold and gold-backed finance occurred later in the 1970s and spans the last three generations of this family business. The turnover in 2022 stood at 1.5 billion dollars. Its phenomenal growth had owed mainly to the more recent developments in the gold market in India.

All these examples hint at a recovery of the state's long engagement with spice, marine goods, cashew, coconut and gold. A completely new form of investment unfolded in the 2000s in fields where human capital advantage joined capital coming in from outside the state.

New Groups, New Fields

With advances in healthcare and medical research, it is not surprising that some of the successful small and medium enterprises of the last twenty years were in healthcare. Investment in this field has happened mainly in speciality hospitals set up by doctors and scientists. One offbeat venture was a well-known pharmaceutical and household chemical company, Jyothy Labs, owner of several popular brands (revenue of 290 million dollars in 2022). Most recent enterprises are in medical equipment and accessories, such as Careon, a surgical and medical apparel maker established by a team of experts; DentCare, the producer of dental care accessories established by John Kuriakose (revenue of 46 million dollars in 2022); and Kanam Latex, a producer of surgical gloves (revenue of 65 million dollars in 2021). Kuriakose started as an assistant in a dental clinic to set up the factory. His biography is used as inspirational material by the company. The start of a biotechnology park near Kochi with easy rules for investments encouraged a few start-ups in this field.

Thomas John started Agappe in 1995 in Mumbai. Agappe is a producer of diagnostic equipment for hospitals. Its expansion came from the reintegration of the Indian economy in the 2000s, when the healthcare industry grew rapidly and became international in the way it modernised and in patient profile. Kerala took part in this transformation in varied ways.

The more unusual case of unconventional business development was IT. As in several other states where IT clusters were created with planned infrastructural investment, the industry cluster in Thiruvananthapuram came up in a Technopark built on the city's northwest edge. The park's origin was a 1990 ministerial visit to the Silicon Valley to explore reindustrialising a state known for an all-round decline in job prospects. The park became functional in 1995. Initially consisting of semi-skilled service providers like data entry firms, the park saw rapid growth in the 2000s. On the eve of the pandemic, the park directly employed about 70,000 people and indirectly employed over 200,000 people. A significant percentage of these workers were women. In turn, IT-led business growth transformed the character of Thiruvananthapuram from a sleepy administrative town into a thriving commercial place served by an international airport. In the 2010s, the town received another hefty dose of infrastructure investment. The Indian Emirati conglomerate Lulu of M. A. Yusuff Ali set up a large shopping mall along a newly minted coastal highway. Gulf money also flowed into hotels.

It should not be surprising that the state will do well in IT. Two of the founders of Infosys, one of the world's largest software companies, Senapathy Gopalakrishnan and S. D. Shibulal, were from Thiruvananthapuram and Alleppey, respectively. The top firms working in Technopark Thiruvananthapuram are almost all multinationals, some with offices in more than one Indian city. At the lower end, there are many struggling and innovative small firms. To help and enable them, some larger groups and the state offer 'incubation' and 'seeding' projects. Venture capital also operates, though it is hard to find systematic data or reports on the scale of such activities.

The boom in IT and related services around 2000 encouraged a tendency already underway in India – private investment in technical education. The state was not behind in the trend. Indeed, Kerala (and south India more generally) has a rich tradition of private investment in education. Many family businesses diversified into this field in the 1970s. A notable example was T.K.M. T. K. (Thangal Kunju) Musaliar hailed from an ancient family of Arab descent and became wealthy as a cashew processor-cum-trader of Kollam in the 1950s. He spent a part of this wealth on setting up an engineering college. The name T.K.M. Centenary (his birth centenary fell in 1997) was later attached to a string of educational institutions.

From that decade, engineering colleges started to deliver engineers to emerging businesses, both in the state and outside. As an assessment done in 2012 showed, there was quick overexpansion. Colleges offered poor-quality education. Some promising students could not join because of the high fees. Faculty recruitment needed to be done with more thought on competence and experience. Some of the graduates had overestimated employment prospects.[30] The study rooted for more public investment, a dubious recipe since public education is known to be cheap but of mixed quality.

Most engineers found jobs outside the state. But those with a general education were absorbed in the service sector, from tourism to construction, retail, and management and consultancy services. These fields forged ahead but under a new identity. Construction has seen a massive boom in the 2000s. A string of large, almost all local companies dominate the private housing business. The biographies of some of the founders suggest that making profits

---

[30] Sunil Mani and M. Arun, 'Liberalisation of Technical Education in Kerala: Has a Significant Increase in Enrolment Translated into Increase in Supply of Engineers?' working paper of Centre for Development Studies (Trivandrum), 2012.

in this business depended on innovation and apprenticeship and not just on managing land and labour, as we may think. In the case of Asset Homes, for example, the core business of apartment building combined with offering a care and insurance package to the buyers. Within a few years in the 2010s, retail was transformed by the entry of superstore chains. V. A. Ajmal, the founder of Bismi, a chain of superstores selling electronics and household goods, was an engineer by training and worked for a trading company based in Dubai before moving into this field in 2003. The Reliance Group's retail arm has recently acquired Bismi. Among management service businesses, Bramma was exceptional. Bramma (Sanjeev Nair) started as a training provider for early career executives, including owners of small businesses. Its clients came from family businesses where the owners were too involved in the day-to-day operations to take time off to reflect on their work. Later, Bramma also supplied management inputs into the operations of businesses like these.

Although remittances did not always drive business investment, foreign contacts mattered significantly and in diverse ways, as we show next.

What Is Special about Capitalism in the State?

The business resurgence had distinct features to qualify as being labelled a New Kerala Model, one built on capitalism. For example, one common thread running through the biographies of leading entrepreneurs in knowledge-based fields is global connections and experience. This was not confined to the Gulf links. Incredible labour mobility and the vast Malayali diaspora contributed to investments in surprising new ways. The international became a business asset in varied ways, often in specific ways. Some entrepreneurs were trained abroad, usually in the United States (US), as scientists and engineers and later diversified into manufacturing products similar to those handled in employment abroad. For example, Gulf-based Malayali businesses invested heavily to dominate the construction boom. Strategic alliances between local and US firms mattered in marketing neutraceuticals and medicines. Again, these deals had a prehistory rooted in the promoter's profile. And finally, businesses such as construction and gold rode on the back of diaspora- and remittance-driven consumption.

There is an additional distinctive feature of the business world. With some exceptions (like Muthoot Finance, Kalyan Jewellers, Agappe Diagnostics), the Malayali capital has an insignificant presence in the rest of India. That does not mean weak ties with the rest of India. Jewellery manufacture and plywood are heavily dependent on migrant workers from eastern India; spice extract firms supply material to health and nutrition brands that have an all-India presence. But as companies or groups, most Malayali businesses remain confined to the state. We read this feature not as a weakness of some kind but as a reflection of deeper integration with the business world abroad, especially that of the Gulf, than other states of India. Capital in the state can generate investment and growth opportunities by relying on ties that most other states have limited access to.

The story in the last quarter century is also one of a significant revival of family capitalism. Corporate and managerial elements played a subdued and dependent role. Like all family businesses in India, it was a hugely male enterprise until the last few years, when a more evenly gender-balanced second generation started taking an active part in management and operations, if not strategy.

Looking at the profiles of expanding companies suggests three processes: (a) the persistence of some old forms of business, revived by the Gulf connection and India's premarket reforms, (b) businesses that built mainly on the inflow of Gulf savings and (c) businesses that were substantially new in profile, which had a profound impact on the domestic workforce and its capability. Although the capital often came from abroad, the workforce employed and sometimes the entrepreneurship had owed to advances in education and mobility of its workers, partially the legacy of the old Kerala Model. But this effect was a minor one as far as one can see.

The first set should include a cluster of firms processing natural resources (seafood, spices, rubber, plywood, coconut and tea). Some were long survivors who did not withstand the generally hostile politics towards big business that prevailed in the 1970s. Some smaller firms did survive on a low key, to grow rapidly with the easing of regulatory restrictions, political restraints on industrial disputes, and access to export markets and foreign technologies. Several that figured in the discussion above were new start-ups. Although much had changed in this field to draw a clear trajectory, the natural resource orientation makes the twenty-first-century re-industrialisation qualitatively like the nineteenth-century boom in trading and manufacturing in the region.

The first set should also include firms originating in more conventional lines of business, like artisanal jewellery, gold trade, and textile trade and production. Again, these fields underwent many ups and downs in the post-independence decades and saw several exits. What we observe now is the cluster that survived and gained hugely from easier policies, access to capital, mobile migrant labour and a shopping boom – all consolidated in the 2000s.

Even anecdotal evidence is insufficient to track how much Gulf money came into conventional businesses in the state. The initial investment in establishing a TMT manufacturing firm in Palakkad (Minar) came from its founder Mohammed Shafi and expatriate Malayali businesspeople. There are a few other examples of direct foreign investment from the Gulf. But on the whole, little Gulf money went into the manufacturing industry. Much more went into services that the middle-class consumers in the state wanted as they grew wealthier. Hotels, restaurants, construction, tourism, shopping malls, healthcare services and filmmaking received such funds. There is no accurate measure of the scale of the inflow.

As the service sector forged ahead, Persian Gulf money moved into services linked to tourism and retail marketing. Several front-ranking Middle East–based Indian-owned groups invested significantly. One of them was Yusuff Ali, an investor in retail marketing (see earlier). A second figure is B. Ravi Pillai, owner of one of the largest engineering firms in Dubai, who invested in retail and hotels in the state. P. N. C. Menon is the owner of an interior decorator company in Dubai with operations both in the Middle East and south India.

Another field where a synergy developed between the diaspora, Gulf investment and domestic economy was the gold jewellery business. Varghese Alukkas started a jewellery trading business in Trichur (Thrissur) in 1956. His son Joy Alukkas expanded the family business in gold jewellery by setting up a showroom in the Gulf in 1987. The intention to capture a part of the massive purchases of gold jewellery by the Malayali diaspora was a great success. With that foundation, the business later expanded in the state and in India. Kozhikode-based Kottikolon Faizal began as a scrap trader, moved to the Middle East, established an iron casting business and invested in hospitals and education in south India, including this state.

Varghese Kurian, the head of a large construction business based in Bahrain, invested in construction, hotels and tourism. Jothish Kumar, the founder of Luker, a manufacturer of electrical goods, had been a senior executive in a white goods multinational, Havells, when he quit to start his brand in LED bulbs and lighting equipment. Muhammad Majeed, the founder of the neutraceuticals producer Sami-Sabinsa, hailed from

Kollam and studied pharmacy in the US in the 1970s. He worked in several pharmaceutical companies, including Pfizer, and finished his doctorate. In the 1990s, he started producing and selling health and nutrition products from the Ayurvedic system. That business grew to become a multinational in the 2000s.

In information and biotechnology, as well as medical and healthcare accessories, we see the third process at work. But more than the scale of capital inflow, the nature of the capital and labour employed in these businesses made all the difference. Some were companies set up and run by professionals, and a break from the family business model that still rules. An educated and significantly female workforce marks another break from the past when women worked in paid jobs to a much smaller extent.

Conclusion

The first thirty years after the formation of Kerala the state saw a failed industrialisation, consisting of two distinct trends: a de-industrialisation in the traditional export-oriented commodity production and the creation of large-scale firms and companies that did not yield value. In the public sector, where most of these had come up, the value added was negative.

This backdrop of failure made the Kerala Model such an attractive idea. It had a biblical message: all those who despair about growth should note that there is hope in human development. The euphoric and clichéd debate that followed left unanswered why the industrial record was so bad. The scholarship on the question processed much data but could have been more persuasive in the explanation. Because most diagnoses lacked a historically rooted explanation, most contributors to that literature had little to say on the recent revival of private enterprise in the state.

The explanation of the whole movement in this chapter follows conventional lines: Kerala lost and rediscovered its comparative advantage. The socialistic path the government of India had chosen to pursue prioritised heavy industrialization based on metals, machines, and chemicals production and discriminated against traditional resource-based industries like the textiles or plantations. Some of these old sectors had been led by foreign firms. These produced jute, tea, coffee, coir, cashew, cardamom and pepper. As the list shows, this region had a lead in producing and exporting many of these commodities. Indian capital dominant elsewhere, the Marwaris and the Gujaratis, took no interest in these businesses and did not understand the complex combination of ecology and globalisation that made these businesses thrive. Capitalism was based on commodity trade under the leadership of global firms that managed that connection. The next thirty years saw a decline in these businesses, not due to a fall in demand but a retreat of capital, enterprise and global connections in marketing, as some of the largest firms left these businesses. The same syndrome of undercapitalisation and debt dependency also plagued the corporate sector. Kerala's lead in non-agricultural business was lost because India's socialist leaders did not like the kind of capitalism that had unfolded in princely Travancore and Cochin.

The revival of capitalism since 1990 happened on the back of natural resource processing as in the old times. But in between, the state had become very different because of the Gulf phenomenon, tourism development and the growth of services and infrastructure necessary for some unconventional businesses to develop. The sources of comparative advantage had changed somewhat. In all fields, value was added by accessing niche export markets or using new technologies. Natural resource extraction does not anymore mean plantations packaging harvested spices but extraction of nutraceuticals. Jewellery manufacture involves invention and experimentation with designs. Rubber products diversified from automotive tyres to surgical accessories.

We do not wish to say that the positive impulses in the last decade or two had owed primarily to corporate capitalism. Even the biggest new industrial firms in and around Kochi would be small compared to the Indian average for medium-sized industries. Few raise significant equity capital or are publicly held. Besides, most service sector enterprises in tourism, trade, transport and real estate are relatively small. Family business remains a strong organisational model. But worrying over size does not make much sense because what counts for economic growth is not the scale of individual business enterprises but the externalities they can generate. From that point of view, a cluster of businesses using locally procured raw materials and skills can have much greater externalities than the public-sector enterprises formed in the state in the 1960s and 1970s.

Foreign investment inflow, which supported business development in the princely areas, was revived simultaneously via the Gulf and IT routes. Neither type of flow can be imagined without significant changes in the prospect of business growth within the state.

The Middle East connection has figured indirectly in this chapter. With labour, it occupies the centre stage, as we see next.

5

Work, Labour and Migration

While advances in mass health and schooling made Kerala quite distinct from other states in India in the 1950s, this was not a pathway to economic and social mobility, let alone economic growth. The quality of education, especially higher education, was poor. The persistence of gender norms kept many women out of the labour force, and high unemployment forced most skilled people out of the state. Outside the state, Malayalis found work, but in jobs that did not provide a dramatic change in conditions compared with similar jobs back home.

The Persian Gulf migration broke the stagnation, not just by offering more gainful opportunities but in indirect, if powerful, ways. In the long run, the job market in the Gulf demanded progressively greater skills from the migrants. Two periodic reports – *India Migration Reports* and *Kerala Migration Surveys* – reveal a trend towards rising skill levels on average, consistent with the diversification of the Gulf economies from oil-based occupations towards financial and business services. Consequently, more jobs opened up in offices in clerical, accounting, sales and supervisory roles. The migration offered those who stayed back in Kerala the scope to invest in human capital. It stimulated growth by increasing construction activity and the consumption of services. It also possibly encouraged business investment, but this link remains under-researched (Chapter 4). A third factor that deserves mention is women's changing roles and economic conditions, both those who stayed back and those who moved out. In both cases, the nature of the migration and mobility link was different from men's.

The recent globalisation, or re-integration with the world economy, is, in these ways, a story of labour – and not primarily trade, foreign capital inflow, or investments abroad. It would still be a mistake to overstress *international* migration or even, more narrowly, emigration to the Persian Gulf. The recent history of labour is also a history of occupational diversification, professionalisation, skill accumulation, shifting gender roles, consumption and saving, and demographic transition.

The present chapter tells that story.

Persian Gulf Migration: A South Asian Story

The Persian Gulf migration occupies such a large and central part of the story that we often forget that it had a prehistory or was not specifically about this place. It is helpful to start with that context.

It is obvious why the movement of people from Kerala to the Gulf is so central a topic. In 2020, about a fifth of the workforce worked outside India. The number of Malayalis working abroad increased from less than 0.1 million in 1981 to 2.4 million around 2014. The number plateaued out around then and then started falling. Migration numbers began to slow in the 2010s due to various factors – emigration from other Indian states, implicit reservation of public-sector jobs for locals in the Gulf markets, and periodic recessions and regulatory tightening in the job market. At its peak, remittances formed a significant part of state domestic income, by one estimate between 10 and 15 per cent in most years.

How did the movement start? The migration of educated Indians and those seeking education had a prehistory. The middle class had been migrating in this fashion for a long time. Going to the port city to acquire higher education was common in the late nineteenth century. There was no essential difference between the princely states and British India in the city's pull upon prospective students and their parents. Little diasporas formed in Calcutta (Kolkata), Bombay (Mumbai) and Madras (Chennai) initially because of this reason, but later also because the migrants stayed on to join city jobs and married into families at their places of origin, which brought many women into the diaspora. Over time, associations that kept alive the memory of their roots cemented the diasporas. Susan Lewandoski wrote how all these processes worked among the Malayalis in Madras city at the turn of the twentieth century.[1]

---

[1] Susan Lewandowski, *Migration and Ethnicity in Urban India: Kerala Migrants in the City of Madras, 1870–1970* (New Delhi: Manohar, 1980).

When oil extraction began in the Persian Gulf region in the 1940s, Malayali workers, already highly mobile within India, went there to work. The connection between India's west coast and the Arab Peninsula through trade, settlement and shipping was longstanding. Mappilas of Malabar, who later migrated in large numbers to the Gulf, were descendants of Middle Eastern settlers on the west coast. The flow to the Gulf continued in the 1950s and 1960s. The numbers were relatively few, and there is little or no record of their experience. But a track already existed when the successive oil price hikes in the 1970s led to a construction boom that demanded hundreds of thousands of workers from abroad. Workers from the state responded more readily than workers from other regions of India.

The enormous scholarly literature on emigration from the state may mislead us into thinking that the story was unique. It was not. Emigration from this region was part of a pan-regional revolution within South Asia that began in the 1970s and continues unabated. Many things the scholars of migration from Kerala discuss or discover were present in other Indian states, in Pakistan, Bangladesh, Nepal and Sri Lanka – all countries that took part in the labour export boom that began in the 1970s. In the state, the effects were concentrated because a larger proportion of the workforce than in most Indian states left home to work abroad. It is still helpful to start with the pan-regional context.

The oil price shocks of 1973 and 1979 had mixed effects on South Asia. The region depended on oil imports and had little capacity to pay a higher price. But as oil revenue and profits were re-invested in the Persian Gulf countries, the demand for workers in construction, utility and other services exploded. Between 1973 and 1985, the number of people living in Bahrain, Kuwait, Qatar, the United Arab Emirates, Saudi Arabia, Oman and Libya rose from a few thousand to several million. Foreign workers came from many regions. South Asia dominated the flow. Pakistan, Bangladesh, Sri Lanka and India were the main source countries. Significantly, the region's youth unemployment rates were higher than the general unemployment rate. With the state's earlier advances in mass schooling, it is unsurprising that people from this region dominated some of these flows.

The migrants were a highly selective population. They were usually educated up to at least secondary school and came from a few regions. In fact, sources were concentrated within the state, a few districts and even a few localities. Migration utilised systems like formal recruitment brokers, personal connections and goodwill, and sometimes extra-legal recruitment agencies – which created a strong link between the worker already there and the prospective migrant. Thus, some groups and districts sent a vast number of men.[2]

Gulf migration generated a substantial remittance flow into South Asia. Immigration rules in the Gulf states made obtaining citizenship practically impossible and made most work contract-bound. The two factors increased the incentive to save and invest back home rather than in the host country. They were usually males in their twenties. 'Across the region, it is often male breadwinners who cross international boundaries', with a corresponding 'feminisation of agriculture'.[3] Women formed about 10–15 per cent of the migrant workers until the end of the 2010s. Sri Lanka and Kerala sent relatively more women abroad but were not significant exceptions to the norm. Although more women stayed back, the fact that the men went abroad changed the economic choices that women faced.

Remittance can, in principle, further stimulate migration by raising expectations. Curiously, even as more people went abroad and more money flowed in, the state's job market was perceived by many who stayed behind as seriously unpromising. 'It is well-known,' a 2007 study quoted the brother of a nurse who worked outside the state, 'that it is difficult to stay in Kerala if you do not have money....'[4] Already, the state's average domestic product was higher than most Indian states. It was not a poor state, but the expected earnings had increased compared with migrant or returned families so much that domestic earnings seemed inadequate. The region had an unemployment problem. But a part of the problem stemmed from this mismatch between average local earnings and expected earnings. A counterpart logic works in the other direction, drawing migrants from the rest of India to the state, as expected wages exceed average wages locally. The force of this mechanism has been felt across all levels of skill. The 'reservation wage' had risen.

[2] Mufsin Puthan Purayil and Manish Thakur, 'The Strength of Strong Ties: Wasta and Migration Strategies among the Mappila Muslims of Northern Kerala, India', *Journal of Ethnic and Migration Studies* 49, no. 19 (2023): 5099–116.

[3] Sanjay Barbora, Susan Thieme, Karin Astrid Siegmann, Vineetha Menon and Ganesh Gurung, 'Migration Matters in South Asia: Commonalities and Critiques', *Economic and Political Weekly* 43, no. 24 (2008): 57–65.

[4] Sreelekha Nair, 'Rethinking Citizenship, Community and Rights: The Case of Nurses from Kerala in Delhi', *Indian Journal of Gender Studies* 14, no. 1 (2007): 137–56, 143.

There were two distinct peaks in the remittance revolution in India. The first occurred during the 1970s and 1980s as the inward remittance in India as a percentage of global remittance flow rose from near-zero to about 8 per cent. A second peak occurred between 1993 and 2015, when the average skill levels of migrants improved substantially and many people went abroad to sell services such as software. In the second peak, the Gulf effect and the participation of Malayalis were weaker.

The pattern of Gulf migration, thus, changed over time as the skill composition of migrants increased in the 2000s. Some people went to start or join businesses in the Gulf. By then, in the source regions, Gulf migration had expanded recruitment agencies, credit and banking, insurance, transportation, trade and services.

The governments of the source countries did not predict or design the flow but welcomed it when it happened. Where bureaucracy once posed obstacles to citizens getting a passport to work abroad, obtaining documents became much easier and speedier. Later, governments participated in negotiations over employment laws and the retrenchment process. More significantly, the governments in South Asia, especially India, recognised remittances as vital support for their shaky foreign exchange situations. Indeed, a region notoriously exposed to foreign exchange crisis could see the end of that instability thanks to inward remittances. A recently published book argues that the Gulf effect stabilised India's balance of payments sufficiently for the government to consider liberalising imports in the 1990s. Earlier episodes of exchange crises had led to more restrictions on imports; in 1991 an exchange crisis had the opposite effect because the government was more confident, and the remittances created the ground for confidence.[5] A key area of financial reform in India – the deregulation of outward remittance – was introduced in response to the surge in inflow in the 2000s.

Until the 1980s, economists and historians would ask why Kerala led the Gulf emigration. After the 1980s, a new question began to be asked: how was migration changing the state? From the 2000s, the growth rate of state domestic product increased. Reviewing a 2002 book taking stock of migration, Prema-Chandra Athukorala said that the scholarship did not probe enough about the emerging 'remittance–growth nexus'.[6] There is now

[5] Tirthankar Roy, *The Economy of South Asia* (London: Palgrave, 2016).
[6] Prema-Chandra Athukorala, 'Review of K. C. Zachariah, K. P. Kannan, and S. Irudaya Rajan, eds., *Kerala's Gulf Connection: CDS Studies on International Labour*

a consensus that while the Kerala Model was growth-neutral, migration was not. The turnaround in the economy owed much to migration and remittance.[7] The link between migration and growth or development operated at four levels – household expenditure, skilling, gender equality and business investment.

Migration and Development: The Consumption–Saving Connection

The wider consequences of migration and remittance would depend on how this money was spent. Remittances had two noticeable effects – improvement in housing and education. The housing effect is the one more easily measurable and possibly the one that took off first. By 2000, a study found the quality of housing among return migrants and left-behind families receiving remittances was significantly better than those without any earning members abroad. A similar effect was present with consumer durables. The former set used more electricity, cooking fuel, cars, television, radio, washing machine and telephone, and, even when relatively poor, were more likely to live in houses with toilets.[8]

Migration and mobility strengthened parental resolve to educate children and equip them for jobs that earned more money than themselves. 'A vast amount of economic capital earned abroad used by the migrant families are invested in the education, health and in the progress of second generation', as in the rest of South Asia sending out people.[9] Remittances created the capacity, expanded the choices and raised ambitions about where to send the

Migration from Kerala State in India (Thiruvananthapuram: Centre for Development Studies, 2002),' *Journal of Asian Studies* 62, no. 4 (2003): 1311–13.

[7] For a review, see Ranjan Aneja and Anandu Praveen, 'International Migration Remittances and Economic Growth in Kerala: An Econometric Analysis', *Journal of Public Affairs* 22, no. 1 (2022): 1–10.

[8] S. Irudaya Rajan, 'From Kerala to the Gulf: Impacts of Labor Migration', *Asian and Pacific Migration Journal* 13, no. 4 (2004): 497–509.

[9] Ginu Zacharia Oommen, 'South Asia–Gulf Migratory Corridor: Emerging Patterns, Prospects and Challenges', *Migration and Development* 5, no. 3 (2015): 394–412; J. K. Parida, S. K. Mohanty and K. Ravi Raman, 'Remittances, Household Expenditure and Investment in Rural India: Evidence from NSS Data', *Indian Economic Review* 50, no. 1 (2015): 79–104.

children for higher studies. This drive shows up in a long and significant decline in labour force participation rates for both men and women, especially women. On the other hand, older women with young children in school who stayed behind took on substantially more duties linked to the education of the children, from arranging tutors and arranging the commute to school to negotiating admissions.

Where did remittances go besides such prominent areas as education and housing on which middle-class households readily spend their savings? Data on investment and saving remains too aggregated to probe this question at a great depth. Non-resident bank deposits increased like in the other states that sent overseas migrants in hundreds of thousands. The conversion of these savings into investments shows an interesting pattern. Unlike the other states where a significant share of the capital went into manufacturing, in this state, a lot of it went into personal (non-housing) loans.[10] There is not yet a satisfactory account of what these loans were for, pending which, it is hard to assess the view that these were 'a problem', meaning that these were non-business investments and 'not job multipliers'.[11]

Remittance changed household labour allocation patterns. For example, there was a general retreat from paid work or 'market work' among those who stayed behind and an increase in self-employment. Remittance inducing a fall in participation in paid employment outside the household is a prominent feature in other parts of the world that experience emigration on a large scale. A study finds that gender and marital status modify the pattern. Married women were more likely to leave paid work for household work, whereas men were more likely to join self-employment.[12] This withdrawal was a reflection partly of the fact that the families could afford such withdrawal in deference to traditional gender roles – but only partly. Women performed different duties at home after emigration took off (see the discussion on women), from financial management to managing children's education.

More recently, with population growth reaching near-zero and a rise in age-related disease and infirmity, remittance has gone into care for the

[10] S. Krishna Kumar and S. Irudaya Rajan, *Emigration in 21st-Century India: Governance, Legislation, Institutions* (New Delhi: Routledge, 2014), 135.

[11] Krishna Kumar and Irudaya Rajan, *Emigration in 21st-Century India*, 136.

[12] M. Imran Khan and C. Valatheeswaran, 'International Migration, Remittances and Labour Force Participation of Left-behind Family Members: A Study of Kerala', *Margin—The Journal of Applied Economic Research* 10, no. 1 (2016): 86–118.

elderly. 'Migrants with their higher spending capacity', a 2022 study finds, 'commonly seek the healthcare services of high-end private "Super Speciality" hospitals for their sick and ailing parents, shifting loyalties from the modest local church-run hospital....'[13] The consumption of speciality healthcare and old-age care has in turn induced a large flow of private investment in the area.

Migration and Development: The Skill Connection

Over an extended period, changing demand for skills at the destination induced the skilling of the potential migrants. That would contribute to economic growth. The link did work, but it worked in a rather complex way. Migration to the Gulf did not, as such, impart skills. Returnees usually moved back to the same occupations they were pursuing before, though there was some capital accumulation in the bargain. 'Work experience abroad, a recent study concludes, 'does not cause any significant upward mobility in any occupational groups except among professionals, who move to managerial positions post-return'.[14] A major study of returnees done in 2021 concluded that about one in five returnees could move into a different or higher-earning occupation after the return. Gulf work did not impart enough money or experience to radically change lives post-reform.

Still, there were indirect and intangible changes. Returnees 'constitute a much more disciplined and committed workforce', for one thing.[15] The infamy that the state nurtured an unruly over-unionised workforce faded away. If the Gulf did not create skills, it demanded higher skills. This effect was strong, and it affected new recruits in the first instance. But as the same recruits returned, their choice of occupations also shifted higher. The composition of the migrants changed constantly in response to demand

---

[13] Sreerupa, 'Transnational Migration, Local Specificities and Reconfiguring Eldercare through "Market Transfer" in Kerala, India', *Journal of Ethnic and Migration Studies* 49, no. 4 (2023): —1014–31' 1024.

[14] Anu Abraham, 'International Migration, Return Migration and Occupational Mobility: Evidence from Kerala, India', *Indian Journal of Labour Economics* 63, no. 5 (2020): 1223–43.

[15] K. C. Zachariah, P. R. Gopinathan Nair and S. Irudaya Rajan, 'Return Emigrants in Kerala: Rehabilitation Problems and Development Potential', Working Paper of the Centre for Development Studies, Thiruvananthapuram, 2001, 4.

for skills in the Gulf, and there was generally a levelling up of skills over time. Those better educated and already in managerial positions were likely to experience a bigger improvement in their conditions than short-term semi-skilled worker migrants.[16] Later studies found that the average skills of migrants rose over time, which was evident from the continuously rising average educational level and remittance in dollars per person, so that the total remittance in dollars continued to rise if more slowly than before.[17]

A new worry emerged. A report conducted in 2011 raised concerns about 'brain drain' and how that was affecting the economy.[18] In the 2000s, as consumers shifted to services, the labour shortage was filled with immigration into the state, where immigrants formed almost half the workforce. On the other side, in the Gulf, the need for semi-skilled manual workers, like those in construction sites, was met not with immigrants from Kerala but from agricultural labour families in Uttar Pradesh and Bihar. Kerala joined the Gulf in supplying work to semi-skilled migrants from the poorer states of India. It is hardly possible any more to discuss emigration as a separate process from the churning of the labour markets in India, the Gulf and this state.[19]

---

[16] P. Azad, A. Abdul Salim and P. K. Sujathan, 'Has Emigration Perked Up Entrepreneurship among Return Migrants in Kerala? Findings from a Survey in a High Migration Density District', *Indian Journal of Labour Economics* 64, no. 5 (2021): 769–86.

[17] K. P. Kannan and K. S. Hari, 'Revisiting Kerala's Gulf Connection: Half a Century of Emigration, Remittances and Their Macroeconomic Impact, 1972–2020', *Indian Journal of Labour Economics* 63, no. 4 (2020): 941–67. Also see Jajati K. Parida and K. Ravi Raman, *A Study on In-migration, Informal Employment and Urbanization in Kerala* (Thiruvanathapuram: Kerala State Planning Board, 2020).

[18] K. C. Zachariah and S. Irudaya Rajan, 'Inflexion in Kerala's Gulf Connection: Report on Kerala Migration Survey 2011', Working Paper of the Centre for Development Studies, Thiruvananthapuram, 2012.

[19] K. Ravi Raman, 'Currents and Eddies: Indian Middle East Migration Processes', *Cambridge Journal of Regions, Economy and Society* 5, no. 2 (2011): 189–205. The 'current' in the metaphor refers to transnational migration, the eddies represent the tighter cycles of internal migration. Migration not only sets the trend for subsequent emigration but also sets in motion a process wherein people occupy the niches vacated by the transnational migrants, thereby purchasing for themselves a new sense of social and economic belonging. In this case, migration not only begets migrants but also feed migrants.

Migration and Development: Women Who Stayed Back

Nearly all the migrants were single or young married males when the Gulf emigration boom started. Forty years on, well over 80 per cent of the migrants were still males. The proportion of women migrants, however, did increase from near-zero to 20 per cent in the first two decades of the twenty-first century. In short, a change set in, but a slow one.

The low proportion maintained over a long time is a puzzle. Women concentrated in agricultural work and handicrafts, which were once organised in factories owned by corporate groups and rich merchants. Both agricultural labour and craft labour declined as craft jobs migrated out of the state. Compensating employment was slow to develop. Why did more women not go to the Gulf? The immediate answer is that most were married relatively early and had young children to look after. Sometimes the jobs required heavy manual labour. Those who stayed back did not necessarily have more economic freedom. Even when women owned or managed land, 'women's role in decision-making [such as the sale of land and use of income] within the economic sphere of agriculture is low'.[20]

The early migration research overlooked women as migrants or members of the families that sent migrants. That changed in the 1990s. In a series of writings, Leela Gulati drew attention to the families with the powerful message that migration profoundly impacted those who stayed home. The number and proportion of women among migrants rose, driven significantly by nursing professionals.

Male migration had an oddly contradictory effect on families. The absence of the men was stressful, yet the remittance and consumption cemented family ties. Gulati showed that mothers and wives sold jewellery to facilitate the migration of men. After the exit of younger men, older members took on more caring duties in the extended family. On the other hand, spouses communicated more than before through letters, thus cementing ties. When remittances started, they stabilised family earnings so the families could plan long-term. The shift was radical in poorer families dependent on casual labour. Children spent more years at school. In families where the male head

---

[20] Shoba Arun, '"We Are Farmers Too": Agrarian Change and Gendered Livelihoods in Kerala, South India', *Journal of Gender Studies* 21, no. 3 (2012): 271–84, 280.

stayed abroad longer, women took on substantially more responsibilities.[21] And finally, migration (predominantly of single young males) may have added to a sharp fall in fertility. Gulati does not offer evidence but argues plausibly that 'migration results in postponement of marriage and prolonged post-marital separation of couples during that critical phase of the life cycle when couples are most fertile'.[22]

By 2000, there were many studies on a class of women who came to be called 'Gulf wives', the wives who stayed behind.[23] Families changed more subtly but profoundly through shifts in women's roles. As parents went on an overdrive to educate children, 'managing the time and energy of children by mothers has become a key component of feminine caring labour', a form of 'affective labour'.[24] Despite its matrilineal antecedents, the society was patriarchal. Younger women entered paid work in large numbers, and older women managed finances and the welfare of their children in new ways in the face of resistance and reactions. None of these patterns was specific to the state or to families sending migrants abroad. Middle-class women across India have taken on more and different roles in the 2000s. The drive to educate children better is universal, and so is an investment in the accessories of a good education. 'Gulf wife' is not a helpful term anymore. But wives in Kerala society may indeed have experienced the transition relatively early and in a more compressed form than in the rest of India.

Migration and Development: Women Who Moved

As female migration levels increased dramatically, the accent shifted away from the stationary Gulf wives in the 2000s. A striking feature of the rise was that, whereas the average age of migrants did not change for men, the average

---

[21] Leela Gulati, 'Migration and Social Change in Kerala', *India International Centre Quarterly* 22, nos. 2/3 (1995): 191–202.

[22] Leela Gulati, 'Male Migration to Middle East and the Impact on the Family: Some Evidence from Kerala', *Economic and Political Weekly* 18, nos. 52–53 (1983): 2217–26.

[23] See Irudaya Rajan, 'From Kerala to the Gulf: Impacts of Labor Migration'.

[24] J. Devika, 'Women's Labour, Patriarchy and Feminism in Twenty-first Century Kerala: Reflections on the Glocal Present', *Review of Development and Change* 24, no. 1 (2019): 79–99, 85.

age of female migrants fell.[25] In other words, whereas, earlier, more women
migrated to join their husbands or to specific tasks requiring experience, such
as nursing, more recently, single girls migrated as students to eventually enter
professions that demanded skills at all levels. The average educational levels of
women migrants were higher than that of men, suggesting that recruitment
for skilled services, which were consumed in greater quantity throughout
the world, had a female bias. For the same reasons (better education and
experience), female returnees seemed to find employment more easily than
men.[26]

Women's migration had a disproportionate impact on the household
than men migration. A study of nurses in Delhi found not only that the
nurses were often the primary earners in their families but also that '[m]
igration often involves a move away from joint family structures to the
nuclear family and singlehood, this offering substantially greater freedom
from family obligations and greater agency and control over their income on
a day to day basis'.[27]

A closer look at the history of the nurses is in order. In the 1950s, overseas
migration, especially to the American job market, got caught up in struggles
over immigration regulations. Women from the region were possibly the
most significant component of the nursing workforce in the industrial towns
of India. For example, the establishments the Tata Group companies owned
in the early twentieth century employed a large number of Malayali nurses
in their hospitals. When the Gulf boom began, the emigration of nurses was
already a common phenomenon in the region. As the state's healthcare system
developed and matured, there was a plentiful supply of trained nurses. Kerala
was ahead of other states in the matter. Nurses not only migrated readily, but
many were also the primary breadwinners for their families.

The Gulf quickly became a large destination for nurses, and a 'new
global map of nurse immigration' emerged.[28] The migration of nurses
increased in scale and aided the growth of institutions like contractor
agencies, private nursing schools and, eventually, bank loan products tailored

---

[25] Krishna Kumar and Irudaya Rajan, *Emigration in 21st-Century India*, 45.

[26] Krishna Kumar and Irudaya Rajan, *Emigration in 21st-Century India*, 61.

[27] Sumangala Damodaran, '"Women" Versus "Breadwinners": Exploring Labour
Market Dynamics, Agency and Identity among Migrant Nurses from Kerala (India)',
Global Labour Journal 4, no. 3 (2013): 186–205, 199.

[28] Reddy, *Nursing and Empire*, 133.

to funding a nursing degree when the aim to go abroad was explicit. The demand for nurses abroad was unstable, being sensitive to immigration policies; therefore, the supply of nurses for the domestic and regional markets was never short. Indeed, the overseas and local markets strengthened one another. The domestic employment sector was a field for 'professionalisation', an organised move 'to raise the educational standards for entry, enhance the status of education, and improve the working conditions and status of its members', which had externalities for employment abroad.[29]

Women also entered the relatively unregulated field of employment, domestic work. Unlike nursing, women's employment as domestic workers comes under the unskilled or 'clearance-required' category of emigration in India. The family (increasingly Indian families) being the employer, domestic work is not regulated by labour laws. And yet, for the individual worker, this is often the most accessible field to enter. All one needs to do is register and pay an agent or contractor who can ease, sometimes bypass, emigration rules. The borderline illegality, overdependence on agents, and absence of rights or rest inside the households gave rise to the impression that such employment exposed the domestic worker to vulnerability.[30] This was an exaggerated concern, for the odd cases of abuse notwithstanding, the flow remained large and growing.

Neither migration nor education significantly improved the position of women relative to men in the local labour market. Female labour force participation rates stayed relatively low in the state, wage disparity between men and women persisted, and females dropped off higher education more readily than men.[31] There were signs that many women withdrew from paid work apparently because they believed the jobs on offer did not do justice to their education, and this proportion was higher among the Scheduled

[29] Stephen Timmons, Catrin Evans, Sreelekha Nair, 'The Development of the Nursing Profession in a Globalised Context: A Qualitative Case Study in Kerala, India', *Social Science and Medicine* 166 (2016): 41–48, 48.

[30] Bindhulakshmi Pattadath, 'The Blurred Boundaries of Migration: Transnational Flows of Women Domestic Workers from Kerala to UAE', *Social Change* 50, no. 1 (2020): 95–108.

[31] Ruchi Bhalla and Surendra Meher, 'Education, Employment and Economic Growth with Special Reference to Females in Kerala', *Indian Journal of Labour Economics* 62, no. 5 (2019): 639–65.

Castes.[32] There was strong indication that whatever the Kerala Model stood for, it did not serve women very well. Not only did higher education or human development not translate into high rates of employment, but the mismatch was greater among women than among men.

Just as the emigration experience encouraged labour agencies and contracting businesses, it also gave rise to invisible social networks. Considerable migration of nurses into Indian hospitals happened through knowledge of which hospital hired which ethnicities of nurses more.[33] This example may suggest that the networks were mainly ethnic or linguistic. They were primarily skill-based and secondarily ethnic. They were present in all levels of Gulf migration, impressions suggest. The networks may have helped develop another migration-friendly skill, learning the language at the workplace. For the nurses working in Delhi, association with other nurses speaking Malayalam would have helped immediately after starting work and in picking up Hindi over a longer time.[34]

Migration and Development: Capitalism

A much less researched link between migration and development was deployment of capital in new businesses. Remittances stimulated consumption and household savings, and, via these, the construction industry. The upturn in growth was first led by construction and then by services. In both cases, remittances played an indirect role. Did it also play a direct role? Did it stimulate the large-scale deployment of capital in new productive investment?

Early assessments were pessimistic: 'Although many go to the Gulf and return with some small savings, few - to the dismay and bewilderment of policy planners - invest in productive businesses,' wrote two anthropologists.[35]

---

[32] Neethu Thomas and D. Shyjan, 'Outsiders of the Labour Force in Kerala: Demystifying Deterrents of Female Work', *Indian Journal of Labour Economics* 65, no. 2 (2022): 445–61.

[33] Nair, 'Rethinking Citizenship, Community and Rights'.

[34] Nair, 'Rethinking Citizenship, Community and Rights'.

[35] Caroline Osella and Filippo Osella, 'Once upon a Time in the West? Stories of Migration and Modernity from Kerala, South India', *Journal of the Royal Anthropological Institute* 12, no. 3 (2006): 569–88, 579.

The general understanding was that the 'multiplier effect' from the additional income was small because the immigrants did not want to take risks with savings and preferred consumption to investment. Much of that negative understanding was conjectural, however.

In the 2010s, the transformation took on a new face, a diversification in manufacturing and skilled services (Chapter 4). There was a better understanding of the remittance–growth nexus, but Athukorala's concern remains timely. While remittances would have stimulated business investment in the state, there is little systematic research in business history on where capital for the newest enterprises comes from and whether the Gulf connection matters there.

Immigration

In the 1980s, it was common knowledge that people from Tamil Nadu were coming to the state in large numbers to work for wages, and several labour-intensive industries had relocated across the border or subcontracted work. In the mid-1990s, a new type of flow began. People from northern India, especially Odisha and West Bengal, came to work in the plywood factories of Perumbavoor near Ernakulam. This was unusual because there were few instances then of northern Indians seeking employment in the deep south. By the end of the 2010s, the flow was substantial and quite diverse in the destination. A study of the plywood industry, where large-scale migration from eastern India first happened, found that employers did not feel happy with Tamil workers, who demanded equal wages and employment conditions with local workers and made frequent home trips.[36]

The census of 2011 showed that interstate migrants numbered less than a million.[37] The first systematic study of the flow in 2013 estimated that

---

[36] Benoy Peter, 'Labour Migration to Kerala: The Case of Plywood Industry' (PhD dissertation of International Institute for Population Sciences, Mumbai, 2010).

[37] Tijo George, Mala Ramanathan and Udaya Shankar Mishra, 'Nature and Composition of InterState Migration into Districts of Kerala: Some Evidence from Census of India, 2011', *Journal of Social and Economic Development* 24, no. 3 (2022): 379–403.

about two and a half million people from outside the state worked there.[38] That figure amounted to over 20 per cent of the labour force, and since most migrants were males, a larger percentage of the male workers in the state. In 2016, the number of migrants was estimated again at two and a half million, consisting of males and females working in construction, hospitality, fishing and farming.[39] Interstate migration continued to be male-biased in recent years, though the proportion of females almost certainly increased with the growth of consumption of services.

Interstate migration on such a large scale raised new concerns over social security and inequality. Recent studies of migrants observe the disparity in wages and living conditions between migrants and locals in similar jobs.[40] An insurance scheme tailored to migrants' needs sought to bridge the gap to some extent and the state recently advanced in protecting the rights of the migrants.[41]

Although the common factor in all cases of migration from the rest of India into the state is the higher expected earnings, the reason and the trigger factor differ from occupation to occupation. An interesting if an offbeat case is gold jewellery, which draws in a large number of Bengali workers. It is offbeat because the making of jewellery involves exceptional skill and expensive raw materials, and, for both reasons, it was traditionally a closely guarded industry where entry for outsider castes was never easy. In the 1990s, reforms in regulatory laws encouraged a massive change in how gold jewellery was made and marketed.

Earlier, only licenced importers of gold could deal in small quantities of the material, confining the business to small local workshops and individual contracts between shopkeepers and consuming families. After the 1990s, the retail business expanded massively, giving rise to large retail outlets in the

---

[38] D. Narayana and C. S. Venkiteswaran, 'Domestic Migrant Labour in Kerala', Gulati Institute of Finance and Taxation, Thiruvananthapuram, 2013.

[39] Divya Varma and Benoy Peter, 'Labour Migration to Kerala: Challenges, Opportunities and Need for an Institutional Response', available at https://www.shram.org/uploadFiles/20170627122555.pdf (accessed 2 February 2024).

[40] Jajati K. Parida, Merry Elizabeth John and Justin Sunny, 'Construction Labour Migrants and Wage Inequality in Kerala', *Journal of Social and Economic Development* 22, no. 4 (2020): 414–44.

[41] See K. Ravi Raman, 'Right-making Is State-making; State-making Is Right-making', Labour Department Policy Series Publications, Government of Kerala, Thiruvananthapuram, 2023, 34–41.

high streets of all major cities. These shops demanded an expansion in the production of the goods and diversification in designs, beyond the capacity of the local shops to cater to. A whole new cluster of workshops emerged to produce goods on contract from retailers, or a new division arose in the older workshops, both employing migrant workers and supervised by a senior worker who spoke the language of the migrants and could keep a watchful eye on them. Migrants did not just accept lower wages than the local workers; they brought the knowledge of a distinct set of designs and products. Most of them came with little skills but were trained in-house by a smaller group of experienced workers.[42]

Conclusion

The migration flow decelerated from the 2010s onwards. There was a positive side to the deceleration. A 2015 study finds that the length of stay in the Gulf varied negatively with self-employment and social mobility prospects.[43] In short, the decision to return did enhance the chance of more economic and social freedom, though the strength of the effect was probably not much.

Early and later workers in the Gulf differed not only in their skills and jobs but also in how migration reorganised their social and cultural lives. Early migrants recreated their milieu at home in the labour camps at their destination. 'The arena of migrant life,' one study based on old photographs found, '[was] predominantly a continuity of pre-existing ties of locality, kinship, community.'[44] These ties weakened over the next several decades. Culturally speaking, the Persian Gulf and Kerala came much closer to one another in the 2000s.

We have explored capital, labour, land and business trends separately. How did these trends add up to growth and development tendencies?

---

[42] Sumeetha Mokkil Maruthur, 'Skill in a Globalized World: Migrant Workers in the Gold Jewelry-Making Industry in Kerala, India', *Journal of Labor and Society* 17, no. 3 (2014): 323–38.

[43] Mathias Czaikay and Maria Villares Varelaz, 'Labour Market Activity, Occupational Change and Length of Stay in the Gulf', *Migration Studies* 3, no. 3 (2015): 315–42.

[44] Mohamed Shafeeq Karinkurayil, 'The Days of Plenty: Images of First Generation Malayali Migrants in the Arabian Gulf', *South Asian Diaspora*, 13, no. 1 (2021): 51–64, 61.

6

Growth and Development

About a decade after India began liberalising its economy, arguments over the best pathway to plan for emerged. Kerala acquired a new significance in this discourse. Did the state have lessons for India at large? The most influential commentators on India's record of human development, Jean Drèze and Amartya Sen, cited the strides in human development, implying that India's policymakers needed to learn lessons from what could be done with limited state resources.[1] A competing view, of which Jagdish Bhagwati was a forceful proponent, said that the accent on human development risked devaluing economic growth. Growth needed competitive markets, which would strengthen the state's finances and sustain the ability to fund welfare and public goods. In this second argument, Kerala was cited as a fiscally unsustainable model. 'The much-advertised model of alternative development, in the Indian state of Kerala,' Bhagwati said in a 2004 lecture, 'with its major emphasis on education and health and only minor attention to growth, had ... run into difficulties....'[2]

How sound were these authors in reading the state's history? Not very, one would think. Bhagwati expressed his pessimistic views even as economic growth had begun to surge. His intuition that the model was unsustainable was probably correct but not testable. Drèze and Sen, writing in 2013, did casually acknowledge that economic growth revived and then attributed it to 'Kerala's focus on elementary education and other basic capabilities', not

---

[1] Jean Drèze and Amartya Sen, *An Uncertain Glory: India and Its Contradictions* (Princeton: Princeton University Press, 2013).

[2] Jagdish Bhagwati, 'Anti-globalization: Why?' *Journal of Policy Modeling* 26, no. 4 (2004): 439–63, 449.

going into the details of how these two things were related.[3] Their discussion of the state's recent history almost totally overlooked the most significant force of transformation, a market-driven one: the export of labour. In short, the market-versus-state choices in the 2000s debate were obsolete tools for a historical analysis of the state.

When discussing that history, what should we be looking at? Chronologically, the first major transformation that marked the state out in India was the positive achievements in education and healthcare, which began in the nineteenth century. The second major transition was the declining average fertility and population growth rates in the middle decades of the twentieth century. Since these topics are much discussed, we will be brief and build on a few major works on the subjects. A third transition that deserves attention is a U-shaped one: deceleration in economic growth in the 1970s followed by acceleration in economic growth in recent decades. Several other chapters in the book contain material that explains what has been going right with investment rates in recent years. Again, this chapter will only briefly touch upon some of these factors. Finally, a fourth theme suggests that despite growth and development in quantitative terms, poverty and inequality persist and have worsened by some measures.

Education

The crux of the Kerala Model was an early and rapid rise in educational levels. The colonial Indian record in primary education was poor, to say the least, though considerable variations existed between regions and communities in academic achievements. The states and districts that later formed the state stood out (Table 6.1).

The search for the historical roots of the unusual educational attainment tends to overplay the state's princely heritage, often reading that heritage wrongly. It is easy to assume that the Indian princes, because they were not British, were more mindful of the welfare of the citizens. There is little evidence and few conclusive ways of testing this proposition because we know so little about the ideologies of the 550-odd states in colonial India. The Travancore kings in the late nineteenth century expressed a progressive outlook, especially on women's education. Still, it is easy to overplay ideology

---

[3] Drèze and Sen, *An Uncertain Glory*, xlii.

Table 6.1 Literacy rate (%)

Year	India	Kerala
1951	27	47
1961	24	55
1971	29	70
1981	36	79
1991	43	90
2001	55	91
2011	74	94
2021	78	94

Source: Census of India, various years; except for the year 2021, *Economic Review*, Government of Kerala.

and miss that the king had more resources than a British Indian province on average. There were many other agents of change in this regard, and some were active well before the rules did.

Whereas most British Indian districts relied on taxes collected from poor peasants living on land that yielded too little per capita output, some southern states like Travancore had a different economic structure and scored significantly more success in raising revenue from the assessment of plantation land, lands growing tree crops and from the pepper monopoly – a joint effect of its geography and attraction for foreign capital. Superior state capacity was strengthened by the fact that the Indian princes received an explicit protection guarantee from British India, meaning they did not need to spend any money on external defence. While they received an implicit subsidy, British India spent an inordinate sum on its army, leaving little for public goods. Not all states, indeed very few, spent serious money on education and health. Madhya Pradesh, Chhattisgarh, Bihar, Jharkhand and Odisha had a high concentration of princely states and an abysmal record of health and education at independence. Travancore did take a road that set it apart from the average. But political ideology alone did not do the job.

The role of the Catholic Church in public welfare is a well-known theme in the scholarship (Chapter 2). The participation of the Catholic Church in public goods dated back to the turn of the twentieth century at least. It increased substantially in the late twentieth century. Between 1965 and 1973, the Church was running more than 800 development projects, including 550 hospitals; it had 840,000 students in its schools; and it received 32 million rupees of foreign aid for development and charity work. The Church also took part in industrial relations and disputes as mediators and encouraged the employment of women workers because they were less unionised, indirectly promoting women's employment.[4] The welfare interest of the Catholic Church was not entirely sui generis. The expansion of Protestant missions added an element of competition.[5] In the long run, the missions pioneered co-educational schools and introduced new forms of female schooling for all religious groups. Female Christian converts also experienced additional educational effects in terms of literacy retention at a later age due to Church practice.[6]

If primary education was a success story, higher education was a story of failure. The state built very few institutions for graduate and postgraduate teaching and research that ranked among the best in India.[7] Successive governments neglected this task and displayed witlessness in meeting the challenge. The truth is primary education can be sustained with government money paying salaries to the teachers alone. Higher education, especially research-oriented fields, can be built with public funds but must be supported by autonomous bodies recruiting faculty. The government is not the ideal agency here. This is so because recruitment for research entails evaluating skills that researchers can deliver better than officers. With weak efforts to either frame a policy or build institutions, higher education saw a proliferation of low-quality colleges and universities built with public and private money.

In recent decades, the consequences of this failure to adapt have drawn much attention. The scale of educated unemployment was the highest among all Indian states. Nearly everybody who gets a college degree even now reportedly struggles to get a job that they are happy with. There are opportunities available for running businesses. Still, these opportunities are

4   P. Neethi, 'Globalization Lived Locally: Investigating Kerala's Local Labour Control Regimes', Development and Change 43, no. 6 (2012): 1239–63, 1247.
5   Tomila V. Lankina and Lullit Getachew, 'Competitive Religious Entrepreneurs: Christian Missionaries and Female Education in Colonial and Post-Colonial India', British Journal of Political Science 43, no. 1 (2013): 103–31.
6   Lankina and Getachew, 'Competitive Religious Entrepreneurs', 125.
7   Justine George and Akhil Menon, 'The Withering of Kerala's Higher Education Sector? Concerns, Choices and the Way Forward', Indian Journal of Human Development, Early view (2023): 1–6.

available unevenly among groups, and relying on business demand can add to inequality.

The paradox is that many universities have empty seats. Prospective students who can, express their view of the college and university system by running away from it. Public universities cannot recruit good faculty because their recruitment system is often politically biased. And private colleges are unwilling to do so. It is common knowledge that many of these colleges sell faculty jobs to the highest bidder. A poorly trained person has the incentive to bid the highest. Privatisation has made great strides. But it worsens the persistent poor-quality syndrome.

Health

Life expectancy at birth was 44 years in 1950 (79 in 2022). India's life expectancy in 1950 was 36 (70 in 2022). The difference between India and Kerala was impressive. Eminent demographers tell us that it did not owe to public goods delivery. Among the larger states of India, Kerala has the most benign environment.[8] Relatively well endowed with moisture and fertile soil and with an average summer temperature well below the north Indian average, the state had never been exposed to the extreme drought events that the Deccan Plateau or even northern, western and eastern India had been subjected to in the nineteenth century or earlier. Therefore, it suffered epidemic outbreaks, especially the four prominent killers, cholera, plague, malaria and smallpox, to a much lesser degree than the drought-prone regions. Droughts and forced migrations made these epidemics spread faster and kill more effectively.

That is not to deny that the princely states made significant advances in basic healthcare and nursing. A solid foundation of local health centres aided immunisation and maternal healthcare drives after the formation of the state. Much of that old infrastructure is still intact. The primary responsibility of the decentralised government offices is to fund and maintain that infrastructure.

---

[8] See Kerala State Council for Science, Technology and Environment, *State of the Environment Report – Kerala 2007: Volume 2, Natural Hazards* (Thiruvananthapuram: Government of Kerala, 2007).

For example, deliveries in a health centre were 87.8 per cent in 1992–93, while the same for India was 25.5 per cent. This has steadily increased over the years, with 99 per cent of deliveries happening in a health centre by 2005 and 100 per cent by 2015, a major achievement in healthcare. This has also been reflected in vaccination, with 80 per cent of children between 12 and 23 months vaccinated by 1999. While the level of full immunisation at the national level was only 44 per cent, it was as high as 75 per cent in the state during 2005. By 2015, the rate further increased to 82 per cent in the state. A National Family Health Survey drive to analyse the expanding services of the Integrated Child Development Scheme (ICDS) survey shows that in the state, 63 per cent of pregnant and nursing mothers utilised at least one of the services, including the supply of nutrition, recreational activities and child development exercises, provided by ICDS. Interestingly, while the relatively well-off social groups, especially religious groups, were reluctant to utilise the ICDS services, historically marginalised groups benefited greatly from these government schemes catering to pregnant and nursing mothers and infants in the state.

Demographic Transition

The state's population history does not stretch further back than the British Indian censuses. In fact, birth and death rates before 1891 are unreliable, if available. As P. G. K. Panikar observed, analysing census data for the three main regions (Travancore, Cochin and Malabar), between 1891 and 1931, the population grew much faster than the rest of India's.[9] The high growth phase began in Malabar later and in Travancore and Cochin earlier. High growth rates imply a fall in death rates, while fertility rates remain high. According to the demographic transition theory, this is the second of three expected phases through which a population tends to move with the broader availability of healthcare, family planning tools, nutrition and jobs for women. Without these changes, death and birth rates are both similarly high, and population growth rates are low. In the third phase, death rates

---

[9] P. G. K. Panikar, 'Fall in Mortality Rates in Kerala: An Explanatory Hypothesis', *Economic and Political Weekly* 10, no. 47 (1975): 1811–18.

had already fallen, and birth rates started to fall, bringing population growth rates down again.

What was the onset of a mortality decline a change from? What was the initial condition like in this region? We do not know for sure. Panikar presumed rather than proved that death rates were high before because epidemic diseases were prevalent. The onset of the second phase meant that the state acted early and effectively to control these diseases. The supply of public goods, in this case, hospitals and health campaigns, by an enlightened princely state delivered a good outcome. A 1984 book strongly claimed that public health worked differently in this enlightened state.[10] The left legacy inherited and strengthened that tradition.

This is not entirely credible and, predictably, a reviewer tore apart the thesis of the enlightened state.[11] Panikar did not have good data to show that the death rates were much higher before and higher due to the same epidemic diseases that caused mass deaths in India. These diseases affected a tiny percentage of the population relative to the rest of India. Kerala did not suffer from droughts, famines and water shortages that could trigger epidemics of cholera and smallpox in other parts of India. Decades that saw so many deaths in India that the population in most parts fell – the 1870s, 1890s and the 1910s – saw net growth in the region. The initial conditions were almost certainly relatively benign, and death rates low. In such benign conditions, a small improvement in nutrition, sanitation and medical care could greatly improve infant and adult mortality. British India needed to go much further to reduce deaths. Public health initiatives (on which only Travancore state left some documentation) were never challenged like in the Deccan Plateau. Sanitation and water quality were less serious issues in this region.

Kerala, in other words, may never have experienced exceptionally high death rates, or the first phase of the demographic transition. Most discussions on public health overlook the extraordinarily benign environment, relatively drought-free and with a low disease load when compared with the north, where

---

[10] P. G. K. Panikar and C. R. Soman, *Health Status of Kerala: Paradox of Economic Backwardness and Health Development* (Trivandrum: Centre for Development Studies, 1984).

[11] Imrana Qadeer, 'Giving Public Health Services More Than Their Due', *Economic and Political Weekly* 22, no. 29 (1987): 1187–88.

every drought brought in its wake an outbreak of infectious diseases because of water shortage and low immunity. That factor alone should explain the state's low death rate and high life expectancy to begin with. Once this is factored in, it remains unclear just what role, if any, public health played in the state that was significantly different from the rest of India. It is also likely that in the first phase, the birth rate was also comparatively low, owing to the lower risk of child mortality and famine and a higher female average age at marriage.

Between 1921 and 1981, average death rates in India had fallen significantly, contributing to increased population growth. In the extent and timing of the fall in death rates, Kerala did not differ much from the all-India pattern. The death rate fell all along the caste spectrum. Again, the state was nothing special. A similar trend was present even in states with a concentration of socially disadvantaged groups. Mothers' education did make a difference in the survival chances of their children, but not by much. The fall in death rates was owed throughout India to the disappearance of demographic shocks due to disasters (famine and disease), nutrition and public health. Since some environmental factors were benign in Kerala, relatively speaking, the agency of public health and nutrition was larger than in India. Health conditions and a late age at marriage of women prolonged women's lives on average, leading to a higher female–male sex ratio.

The third phase of the demographic transition starts with a decline in fertility rates. In 1981, the population density in the state (at 654 persons per square kilometre) was three times that of India's. Many adults were, by then, migrants or seeking jobs outside the state, but their number was nowhere near the scale needed to make a difference in population density. What made a difference was not migration but average birth rates. The birth rate had started to fall more rapidly than in India. This was the unusual nature of the state's demographic transition, an early and faster decline in birth rates. A drop in birth rates probably began in the region in the 1950s, before family planning methods became widely available and population control became a campaign point for national policy (1970s onward). Since 1981, population growth rates have decelerated in the state faster than in India (Table 6.2 and Figure 6.1).

What had led to that change? In early discourses on the Kerala Model, scholars explained the onset of the fertility decline with reference to the public health system and the fall in infant mortality rates, the much larger system of primary education in the state, and the relative rarity of child employment. Extensive primary education encouraged competition among parents to educate their children. These factors would make it attractive to

Table 6.2 Population 1901–2011 (million)

Year	Kerala	Indian Union
1901	6.4	238.4
1911	7.1	252.1
1921	7.8	251.3
1931	9.5	279.0
1941	11.0	318.7
1951	13.5	361.1
1961	16.9	439.0
1971	21.3	548.0
1981	25.4	683.3
1991	29.1	846.4
2001	31.8	1,028.7
2011	33.4	1,210.7

Source: Census of India, various years.

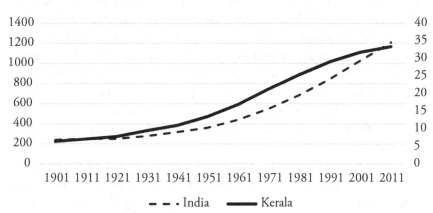

Figure 6.1 Population, Kerala (right axis) and India in millions
Source: Census of India, various years.

parents to adopt family control methods when these became widely available. Parents in the state were pioneers in this process.[12]

---

[12] P. R. Gopinathan Nair, 'Decline in Birth Rate in Kerala: A Hypothesis about the Inter-Relationship between Demographic Variables, Health Services and Education', *Economic and Political Weekly* 9, nos. 6–8 (1974): 323–36; P. G. K. Panikar, 'Fertility

Not disputing that education and health mattered, the argument is not wholly persuasive. If, as we argue above, the death rate was partly geographically determined to be low in the region, infant mortality must have been low from the start. There is insufficient data on the initial conditions to tell how low it was. In that case, the fertility rate was an endogenous process, a response to a fall in disease loads as in the rest of India, and not generated either by public health or educational advances. The scarcity of child employment is an ambiguous thing. It could be the effect of a relatively smaller agricultural sector in the region due to its geography. Kerala was luckier than prescient with the demographic transitions. Women in the state married later than women in India on average. The gap was large enough to suggest why fertility rates were smaller than the Indian average. But the age of marriage was rising in both Kerala and India, roughly at a similar pace. It would not fully explain the divergence in fertility decline.

In theory, a population shift from labour-intensive agriculture to capital- and skill-intensive urban services and industry might reduce the value of having many children and strengthen the drive to educate fewer children better. The logic does not work for the state all that well. Although the workforce was overwhelmingly rural (not concentrated in isolated villages), it was not overwhelmingly agricultural. While the state had invested heavily in education, it had underinvested in higher and technical education, offering limited opportunities for skill-building and diversification of jobs. That failure may have raised the cost of educating children too high. But the effect would be limited to a few families. Most would not be able to think of (not at least in the 1970s) educating children in sophisticated skills while staying inside the state.

Some scholars (like K. C. Zachariah) attributed the fertility decline to politics, especially the radical land reforms of the 1970s. The land reforms made the landed elites more concerned about shifting their children away from dependence on the land and the poorer sections of society more mindful of the possibility of catching up with the elites. Either way, the value of education increased. The logic is not perfectly testable. Some of the transitions implicit in this argument – educational enrolment, for one – preceded the land reforms.

Decline in Kerala: Social Justice Hypothesis', *Economic and Political Weekly* 19, no. 13 (1984): 571–72.

One relevant point to note is that, controlling for adult female literacy and the religious composition of the population, Kerala was no different from patterns observable in adjacent districts in Tamil Nadu and Karnataka. Rather than the state's unusual social or human development experience, something else prevailing in a large part of southern India had worked to cause the early fall in birth rates. One of these factors was a joint outcome of public policy and commercialisation – the easy availability and widespread awareness of contraceptive methods.

For some time now, a fourth demographic transition has been underway in the state: the ageing of the population. It is beginning to generate serious scholarly interest. With population growth falling below replacement since 2001, the population is ageing faster. In 2013, the Centre for Development Studies published a Kerala Aging Survey. The report and the subsequent studies revealed many unknown sides of a growing challenge.[13] One of the new findings was that the rapid ageing of the population was a joint outcome of a fall in birth rates and migration of the working-age population. In other words, more and more older people are left to look after themselves. This complicates the task of building systems of care. Another significant trend was the growing anxiety among older people about the well-being of their children, who live far away and often struggle to build a secure life for themselves.[14]

Growth and Structural Change

Figure 6.2 shows economic growth by a standard index (per capita income). The values were below the Indian average in the 1980s. From the 1990s, there was a turnaround, at first modest and then, in the next decade, quite a sharp one. Table 6.3 on structural change suggests where the growth is concentrated. The broad trends of structural change were quite similar between the state and India – a fall in the share of agriculture, a modest rise in the share of manufacturing, and a sharp rise in the percentage of the

[13] S. Irudaya Rajan, Aneeta Shajan and S. Sunitha, 'Ageing and Elderly Care in Kerala', *China Report* 56, no. 3 (2020): 354–73.

[14] Julie Abraham, Sibasis Hense and Elezebeth Mathews, 'Changing Social Dynamics and Older Population: A Qualitative Analysis of the Quality of Life among Older Adults in Kerala', *Journal of Geriatric Mental Health* 9, no. 1 (2022): 34–42.

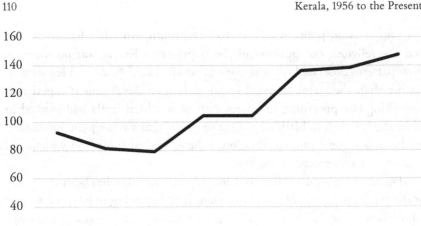

Figure 6.2   Per capita income (constant prices) of Kerala as a percentage of all-India, 1980–2013

Source: https://www.ecostat.kerala.gov.in/ (accessed 20 February 2024) and Central Statistical Office, National Accounts.

Table 6.3   Sector shares in domestic product (%)

Year	Kerala			India		
	Primary	Secondary	Tertiary	Primary	Secondary	Tertiary
1970	33	13	54	45	19	36
1980	31	17	52	39	21	39
1990	25	19	55	30	20	50
2000	20	21	58	29	20	51
2010	16	22	61	18	27	55
2020	13	24	63	18	25	57

Source: https://www.ecostat.kerala.gov.in/data-subset/207 (accessed 2 February 2024).

tertiary sector. The difference was that agriculture's share fell much faster in the state throughout the timespan shown in the table, and manufacturing's share increased faster than in India.

The long-term trends cannot be explained simplistically with Drèze and Sen's formulation: 'focus on elementary education and other basic capabilities' generated recent economic growth. The relationship between capability and growth was not straightforward and there is no direct evidence that these factors played a role behind the average income trend. If that were the case, we would not see the relative decline in the 1970s, when the state was still ahead of all-India averages in 'basic capabilities'. We need to explain the decline and reversal primarily with reference to a fundamental market process: the profitability of private investment. As Chapter 4 on business conditions showed, the decline in economic growth was owed to the attrition of private investment in traditional industrial sectors and perhaps the withdrawal of investment from agriculture after land reforms. By the same logic, the revival reflects a return of private investment. Let us see what the national accounts data show.

In 2020, the share of the secondary sector, and of manufacturing within it, was roughly similar between India and Kerala. The share rose faster in the state in the previous twenty years than in India. That suggests a re-industrialisation process in the state that has received surprisingly little attention. The striking difference was in agriculture and the tertiary sector. The share of the primary sector was significantly smaller in the state than in India (in 2023, 8 per cent compared with 18 per cent for India), and the share of the tertiary sector significantly higher (in 2023, 63 per cent compared with 53 per cent for India). In the last fifteen years, the share of the government or public administration stayed constant at less than 5 per cent. The driving force of the state economy has been private services, which have posted higher growth rates than the Indian average and increased their share, especially trade, transport and real estate. In 2023, each one of these heads had a larger share of income when compared with India. To sum up, the resurgence was primarily services-led; manufacturing revival made a modest secondary contribution.

If a state like Kerala experiences positive economic growth, three possibilities come to mind. First, foreign inward remittance fuelled consumption of services. But this hypothesis is not credible because inward remittance in dollar terms has stagnated since the mid-2010s. The second hypothesis is that investment as a proportion of state income has risen. Based on fixed capital formation data, that does not seem to be the case. Fixed capital formation as a proportion of domestic product is about half that of India (in 2015, 20 per cent as against 40 per cent in India and, in 2018, 16 per cent against 30 per cent in India). Throughout the 2010s, the investment ratio in the state and that in India maintained a stable relationship. Both percentages rose in the early 2000s and fell slightly in the 2010s. Infrastructure investment has risen in the state in the last few years. Again, Kerala may not be an exception in that respect.

A third possible explanation is that investment took the form of human capital formation, which the fixed capital dataset cannot capture. Investment in services is embodied in the skills and capabilities of the people employed. The capital formation dataset can only measure investment in construction and machinery. Thus, if a hospital buys new instruments, then that will count as fixed capital formation, but if a hospital hires doctors specialised in new treatments at high salaries, then that expenditure will not count as capital formation. That, of course, makes no sense in a state where private healthcare has forged ahead faster than in the rest of India. Gross fixed capital formation data consistently underestimate investment in services. Most of the fixed capital formation takes place in manufacturing, agriculture and real estate, where assets are counted. Trade and transport contribute little to fixed capital, even though they generate more income growth.

To conclude, it appears that human capital formation did play a role, but how prominent or sustainable that role was we cannot say without more research on the services. Does this confirm Drèze and Sen's formulation that 'elementary education and other basic capabilities' generated a turnaround? Not quite. This is not a story about 'basic' capabilities, but specialised business-oriented capabilities that generated monetary returns. It is a different story, one scripted by private spending, not public spending.

The migration history did contribute to the turnaround, but in highly indirect ways in recent years. Income received through remittance went initially into construction and consumer durables (Chapter 5). Consumption shifted from inferior goods to normal or even luxury goods. The service sector expansion reflected the shift in part. Sectors like banking and finance, trade and hotels, real estate, tourism-related services, education and private healthcare, including specialist care and hospitals, gained from the inflow of money. Increased income also resulted in high savings, which contributed to investments. Finally, as Chapter 4 has shown, migration enabled the emergence of industrial entrepreneurs who had either made their money abroad or had gained technical experience abroad. To this mix, India's neoliberal reforms added another factor. By reducing trade restrictions, the reforms allowed an emergent cluster of medium-scale enterprises to utilise the state's natural resource advantage better than before.

Public Finance

As the turnaround matured, other processes, again market-mediated, contributed to it. One of these was a more stable public finance. A second one was the consolidation of women's agency (see next section). And a third one was the ability to draw private investment from outside the state into new businesses like information technology (Chapter 4). It is almost certain that the infrastructure investments the state undertook and the availability of a skilled services workforce were attractions for investors who came into the state.

Between 2004 and 2014, tax revenue in the state increased substantially. Much of that increase reflected increased collection from transaction taxes like the sales tax, the most direct way economic growth adds to a state's revenue. More than three-quarters of what the state earned went into committed expenditures like salaries of administrative personnel, leaving little for infrastructure or development. However, the improved financial situation made the state more creditworthy, leading to credit-financed capital projects.

Still, the core responsibilities of the state in healthcare and education drew in most of the developmental expenditures. Only now, the local governments were responsible for a significant proportion of these expenditures. In 1994, a year after a constitutional amendment, Kerala had embarked on local self-governance through elected councils called *panchayats*. Theoretically, these local bodies could raise taxes mainly via property and professional taxes. And the pressure from below would ensure that the money was spent on local development. This was undoubtedly a radical reform and was hailed as such in the early 2000s.

The *panchayats* did raise substantially more money in 2004–15, thanks not so much to the reform but to the availability of more money to tax. It remains doubtful if the move impacted the state's capacity to raise taxes locally and invest the funds in local development. An overview done around 2017 did not think the impact was dramatic or revolutionary.[15] The *panchayats* remained more, not less, dependent on grants from the state government and, therefore, functioned with little autonomy, political or fiscal.

---

[15] M. A. Oommen, Sally Wallace and Abdu Muwonge, 'Towards Streamlining Panchayat Finance in India: A Study Based on Gram Panchayats in Kerala', *Economic and Political Weekly* 52, no. 38 (2017): 49–58.

In the 1990s, the electricity industry was subjected to significant reforms throughout India. The broad trend was 'unbundling' generation and distribution, partial privatisation and a move towards interstate trading in energy. Kerala benefited greatly from the reforms, especially the last one. Its generation system is heavily dependent on hydroelectric power. In common with the drier Deccan Plateau, the state has built eighty-odd dams since the 1950s to generate power and store water for consumption and irrigation. Rich in fast-flowing rivers, the region had considerable scope to build such projects. However, hydroelectric projects yielded a seasonally variable supply, much below the total needs. And no major project could be started in this field because of opposition from environmentalist groups.

With the resurgence of growth, demand grew as commercial services exploded in the state (by contrast, industrial and agricultural uses were relatively low, at about a quarter of the total consumption in the state). At the same time, anxiety about overdependence on external sources grew. It is not feasible for the state to generate coal or natural gas power. The only option left for local generation is renewable energy, especially solar and wind, and building larger storage systems. A policy-framing body that had existed since 1986 received a new relevance from two sides: energy policy and climate change. There was some scope to build synergy between local government and local generation and trade of power. Transition to net zero, in this way, entailed projects on expanding hydro, solar and wind energy.

Women's Agency, Poverty and Inequality

The state's female literacy rate, 36 per cent, was well above the national average in 1951. It increased to 92 per cent in 2011. This was a significant rise, though the national average rose even faster, from 18 to 73 per cent in the same years. The gap between male and female literacy narrowed at the same time. Female life expectancy, similarly, saw a large rise, but again, India's rate nearly caught up with it. Although more educated than before, women, especially urban women, have registered a rather low work participation rate since the 1980s. A part of this pattern would owe to the preference for higher education. But the migration of male members might also explain some withdrawal of women from the workforce.

Women's participation in the household decision-making process, however, increased over the years. It is not clear if this change was due to political empowerment and awareness of rights, migrant remittances that women control, or participation in the labour force. In any case, the ratio of women with money at their disposal increased in the 2010s. More Hindu (45 per cent), Christian (46 per cent) and Scheduled Caste (43 per cent) women spent their own money as they wished than the state average. This figure came down to 27 per cent for Muslim and Scheduled Tribe women each. Parallel to this, women's participation in decision-making increased from 47 per cent in 2005–06 to 68 per cent in 2015–16 in the state.

According to the various expert groups appointed by the Planning Commission from time to time to review and evaluate poverty, poverty in India fell from 59 per cent in 1973–74 to 7 per cent by 2011–12. The state's poverty level fell from above the Indian average to well below it.[16] Measured by the 'multidimensional poverty index', poverty was as low as 0.55 per cent (2019–21) in the state. A similar picture shows with monthly per capita expenditure (MPCE) calculated from time to time. The MPCE stood far better than the national average, and was at the top for most years since 2000. All communities did not experience a reduction in poverty to an equal or similar extent. Poverty among Scheduled Tribe groups was higher than any other community (39 per cent in 2012). The extent and speed of reduction were much smaller for these groups.

These differences suggest that inequality was (and remains) persistent, especially between broad social groups. National Sample Survey reports over the years reveal a significant consumption inequality between different categories of people. This is true for both rural and urban areas. If taken as a proxy for income, a clear division existed between different communities and their counterparts in urban areas.[17] The growth in income was higher in urban areas and among communities belonging to higher strands of social ladders. Although all communities experienced a boost in their income, it was not uniform, with several communities faring better than the others. As

---

[16] Government of India, *Report of the Expert Group to Review the Methodology for Measurement of Poverty, Planning Commission* (New Delhi: Government Press, 2014).

[17] The monthly per capita consumption of Scheduled Tribe communities in urban Kerala in 1999–2000 was 994 rupees, which was higher than all other communities in rural Kerala. This fact does not fade away as we move to 2011–12, where the consumption of these communities in urban Kerala (3,389 rupees) was still higher than that of the general community in rural Kerala (3,165 rupees).

mentioned, the rural–urban divergence in the extent of income growth was also significant (data relates to 1999–2012).

In recent years, the income difference between the lowest and top classes has remained high in both rural and urban areas.[18] Systematic and considerable differences existed between the Scheduled Caste category and the general population and the Other Backward Classes category and the general population. Keeping in mind that consumption as a percentage of income was higher for low-income households and lower for high-income households, this difference between income and consumption could be much higher than what we can anticipate. Although the relative prosperity of the marginalised communities was far better than their counterparts in other parts of India, there existed an inequality in consumption between the communities. There was a visible difference in rural and urban consumption in general. This is important, as most of the backward communities were marginalised in the rural areas. Most of the backward communities who resided in the rural areas failed to gain from the revival of growth as much as the others did. To the extent these groups continued to rely on land, the minimal entitlements to land that they had contributed to their poverty and the slow improvement in conditions. Even now, in the villages, higher landholdings indicate better economic conditions.

The National Sample Survey data for 2009–10 shows that the land possessed by the bottom 60 per cent of the population was just 9 per cent, while for the top 15 per cent, it was more than 70 per cent. The former had seen a rise in landholding share but it was very marginal. Eighty-two per cent of the Scheduled Caste population lived on the land they inherited. Limited mobility and land dependence reinforced mutually, implying limited mobility of Scheduled Caste communities. A similar inequality existed in the average value of assets per household in rural areas. The National Sample Survey 70th round on debt and investment (2013) shows that the average asset value per household is increasing as one moves from lower deciles to higher, both in rural and urban areas.[19] The debt to asset ratio (DAR), which is the average amount of debt outstanding on a given date for a group of households expressed as a percentage of the average value of assets, was

---

[18] Government of India, *Report of the Expert Group to Review the Methodology for Measurement of Poverty, Planning Commission*.

[19] Government of Kerala, *Debt and Investment in Kerala* (Thiruvananthapuram: Department of Economics and Statistics, Government of Kerala, , 2013).

high among the families with low levels of assets, or the lowest deciles of asset holding. On the other hand, reflecting creditworthiness, household indebtedness is high among the top deciles of asset holders.

Inequality persisted in the expenditure on capital too. Only 8.7 per cent of the bottom decile spent on fixed capital except land, while the figure was 23.5 per cent in rural Kerala. The bottom decile did not spend money on buying land, while this was around 3.3 per cent for the top decile. In urban areas, while a mere 6 per cent spent money on fixed assets and 4.1 per cent on buying land, for the top decile the proportions were 19.7 and 0.1 per cent, respectively. Not only was the asset inequality staggering, but more and more assets were being bought by the top asset-holding households in the 2010s.

Inequality also persists in primary indices of human development. The fertility rates among different communities are not similar. The total fertility rate (TFR) of Hindus is lower than that of other categories such as Muslims, Christians and Scheduled Castes. On the contrary, the TFR of Scheduled Tribes is far higher than the population replacement ratio of 2.1. Given that fertility ratios are influenced primarily by social parameters like education, health and financial development, the high fertility ratio among the Scheduled Tribe community suggests that social development has been uneven. Infant mortality rates, which have declined to a significant extent, were higher in rural areas (5.2 per cent) than in urban areas (3.5) in 2021. Malnutrition is higher among households in the lower quantiles while the same reduces as we move up to the higher quantiles. While half of the children in the state's lowest two quantiles (50 per cent) have stunted growth, it reduces to 18 as we move up to the high-income quantiles. In turn, these differences reflect the consumption inequality discussed earlier. Similar differences persist in literacy, enrolment and school dropout rates.

Conclusion

The hallmark of the Kerala Model was easy and cheap access to primary education and healthcare. The state remains a distinct entity and way ahead of most Indian states in ensuring such access even to the poorest people. It is not true, however, that these factors alone explained the state's demographic trajectory. The trends in Kerala and India were more similar than different.

Over the last three decades, the primary driving force sustaining education and healthcare has shifted from the public to the private sector.

Migration, investment and the resurgence of capitalism ensured that the market would take over social well-being, leaving the state in charge of addressing environmental issues, inequality and infrastructure. Improved public finances and greater creditworthiness added force to that tendency.

Concern over inequality is perhaps the most enduring legacy of the left movement in the state. This has not gone away, but the left needed to reinvent itself as a market-friendly force to serve that aim in more recent times. The popularity of the communist parties, even as the movement suffered a fall worldwide, owes to this dual process. We turn to this issue in the next chapter.

7

The Left Legacy

For years now, Kerala has had the distinction of being ruled by a communist-party-led coalition. The communist alliance won the first state assembly elections in 1957, lost in 1960, returned to power, and ruled the state in 1967–70 (first under E.M.S. Namboothiripad till 1969 and then under C. Achuthamenon), 1970–77, 1978–79 1980–81, 1987–91, 1996–2001, 2006–11 and since 2016. In between, there were years when the state was under President's Rule, that is, the federal government governed it. The composition of the left coalition changed. It was never a body consisting of only the ideologically left parties: the Muslim League and some Christian factions allied with the communists. However, the main constituents of the coalition were the Communist Party of India (CPI) until 1964 and the CPI (Marxist), or CPI(M), after the CPI split into two parties.

In no other state of India, except West Bengal (and later Tripura), did the CPI or CPI(M) command a popular support base large enough to win elections. In common with West Bengal, tenants and agricultural labourers in these acutely land-scarce regions formed the main support base for the party. The communists won elections on the promise of land reforms. There was another historic factor behind their popularity. Caste equality movements coalesced around the leftist movement. Because of their commitment to the rural and land-dependent poor, the left delivered land reforms in Kerala and West Bengal in the 1970s. And in both states, ruling left parties indirectly drove private capital out of trade and industry. Ideological differences within the Communist Party of India led to a split in 1964. A faction led by S.A. Dange tended to have cooperation with the Indian National Congress, which then had a good relationship with the Soviet Union. That and the debates on National Bourgeoisie led to the split.

This is not a paradox. The paradox was that from the 1990s, if not earlier, the left quietly turned friendly towards private capital. By then, agriculture was in retreat, the old base of the left was not significant anymore, and the state was rapidly falling behind India in economic growth (and investment rates). The reinvention was a dramatic success. Even as Marxist parties sank in West Bengal, the left returned to power with a significant majority in the 2021 elections, the first time since the formation of the state that a sitting government in the state was elected for a second consecutive term. The recent capitalist resurgence was crucial to the popularity of the left. As the private sector took charge of investment, and even education and health, the state could afford to focus on decentralised governance, corruption-free administration and urban infrastructure.[1] The class-based politics of the 1960s and 1970s was dead. With private investment rising, the state had more capacity to fund public administration.

The present chapter is a chronological account of this unfinished transition.

The First Left Government

In the 1957 election, the first in the state, the CPI, with independent candidates, led a government with a slender majority. In terms of vote share, the Congress had the highest percentage with 39 per cent, followed by the CPI with 35 per cent, the Praja Socialist Party with 11 per cent and the Revolutionary Socialist Party with 3 per cent. The CPI won 60 seats and with the support of 5 independent members, formed the first ministry. Some of the independent candidates drew votes that later went to the Muslim League, which was not yet a recognised party.[2]

---

[1] K. Ravi Raman, 'The Opposition "Emocracy" Exposed: Kerala's Landmark Left Victory', *Monthly Review*, 15 October 2021, https://mronline.org/2021/10/15/the-opposition-emocracy-exposed-keralas-landmark-left-victory/ (accessed 4 February 2024). With the redefined role of the Kerala Infrastructure Investment Fund Board (KIIFB), after the left-led Pinarayi Vijayan government came into power in 2016, the state has accelerated infrastructure investments expecting output multipliers.

[2] T. J. Nossiter, *Marxist State Governments in India: Politics Economics and Society* (London: Pinter, 1988); P. M. Salim, *The First Popular Government in Kerala and Liberation Struggle – 1957–59: A Historical Study* (Calicut: University of Calicut, 2013). Though communist activities had been taking place since the early twenties,

Chief Minister E. M. S. Namboodiripad had promised agrarian reforms in his election manifesto.[3] The state initiated an Eviction of Tenants Act, administrative reforms and an education policy. On 5 April the party assumed power, and on 30 April the revenue minister K. R. Gouri presented the historic Kerala Stay of Eviction Proceedings Bill of 1957, which the Legislative Assembly later passed on 8 May. This was the first enactment of a land reform law in the state's legislative history and the beginning of the road to redistribution-based land reform that would come in 1970. The 1957 act prohibited all evictions of tenants, sub-tenants and occupants of homestead land on any ground, including failure to pay rent. Court proceedings initiated by landlords against tenants were also stayed with immediate effect. Two front organisations of the CPI, the Kisan Sabha and the Agricultural Workers Union, which had since the mid-1930s represented the peasants and workers, respectively, directly intervened to stop all evictions.

This was a dress rehearsal for the Kerala Agrarian Relations Bill, 1957, which the Assembly passed on 10 June 1959. The bill had the provision of granting a tenant fixity in tenure, a fair rent and ownership. This bill also had provisions for applying ceilings on surplus land holdings and the distribution of land. Significantly, this bill restored the land rights to tenants who were evicted after the passing of the Stay of Eviction Proceedings Act. This was followed by the introduction of the Kerala Agrarian Relations Bill (KARB). Revenue Minister Gouri introduced the bill in the assembly on 21 December 1957, which was later passed by the assembly on 10 June 1959. Though the chief minister expressed hope of getting the approval of the President, a struggle launched by the opposition parties and the foreign-owned plantation lobby against KARB and the Education Bill (see later) led to the dismissal of the government and President's Rule in the state. In the following election (1960), the CPI could not form a government despite winning a slightly larger

---

with the formation of Congress Socialist Party in 1934 and the Parapram–Pinarayi meeting of 1939, the movements gained momentum. The Communist Party was banned in 1948 until 1952. CPI won 29 seats in the election to the assembly of the Travancore-Cochin and in 1954. In Malabar, the CPI won 13 seats and the party increasingly began to reinforce electoral politics for the communists.

[3] C. Achuthamenon, 'Keralathinoru Masterplan', pamphlet published by Prabhat Book House, Thiruvananthapuram, 1957; E. M. S. Namboodiripad, *The Communist Party in Kerala: Six Decades of Struggle and Advance* (New Delhi: National Book Centre,1994).

vote share than before. The Congress and Praja Socialist Party government passed land reforms in 1961 and 1963 after diluting the provisions.

Land Reforms

The left returned to power in 1969. Radical land reforms were back on the agenda (see also Chapter 3). The Kerala Land Reforms (Amendment) Act, 1969, was implemented after a series of amendments and discussions to abolish the tenancy system. The Kerala Agrarian Relations Bill (KARB) passed by the first communist ministry in July 1959, for instance, was silent on the question of Adivasi land rights; it also exempted private forests from ceiling provisions. Although it claimed that foreign-owned plantations would be nationalised, this was not done. The possibility of releasing surplus land in the high ranges, which would have brought some relief to the landless Adivasis and the plantation workers, was forestalled.

Two radical steps discussed in 1957 – the application of ceilings on holdings, at least concerning foreign-owned plantations, and the acquisition and redistribution of surplus land – had met with failure.[4] Surplus land was initially estimated in 1957 at around 1.7 million acres. It declined to 0.1 million acres in 1964 and went further down after 1970.[5] It is not clear exactly how the surplus disappeared from the accounting. Marxist scholars predicted that a fragmentation of the estates would be an economically counterproductive move. It would be practically impossible to induce the peasants in the lowlands to move up to the highlands. Some scholars, however, argue that this was a way to avoid difficult questions about class and caste inequality.[6]

The 1969 act vested ownership rights to the tenants over their cultivated land, conferred them the rights to purchase land around their dwelling at a minimal rate and placed a ceiling on land ownership wherein the surplus land was used for distribution. Under the act, over four million applications were

---

[4] K. T. Rammohan, 'Understanding Kerala: The Tragedy of Radical Scholarship', *Monthly Review* 43, no. 7 (1991): 18–36.
[5] P. Radhakrishnan, *Peasant Struggles, Land Reforms and Social Change: Malabar 1836–1982* (New Delhi: Sage, 1989).
[6] K. Ravi Raman, 'Breaking New Ground: Adivasi Land Struggle in Kerala'. *Economic and Political Weekly* 37, no. 10 (2002): 916–18.

filed to confer land rights. A total of 0.17 million acres of land was considered surplus land available for distribution. However, about a quarter of this was exempted due to court interventions or disputes. A little less than 0.1 million acres were taken over for distribution.[7]

In 1971, Chief Minister C. Achuthamenon and Revenue Minister Baby John introduced the Kannan Devan Land Resumption Bill. The bill was to acquire the uncultivated land under the formerly British-owned Kannan Devan Company for distribution among the landless workers in the state. Baby John reiterated the argument that the land under the company was originally the government's that was leased to the company. Of the 135,000 acres of land managed by the company, the government acquired 25,000 acres of land for redistribution. The exact amount of land that was then redistributed remains unclear. The land remaining with the three major private plantations, Kannan Devan, Harrison Malayalam and Malayalam Plantation, amounted to 93,000 acres, much larger than the land distributed under the land reforms. Vast chunks of plantation land remained uncultivated and undistributed.

Half of the land in 1970 was under the tenancy system. Given a very high person–land ratio, the land that was given via redistribution was about 0.8 acres per tenant. By the beginning of 1980, 3.4 million applications were filed to transfer land rights from landlords to tenants. Of these, 2.4 million applications were allowed, and the rest were disposed of or settled.[8] The Land Reform Review Board was established in the same year to oversee the efficient implementation of land reforms. This was supervised and monitored by the Land Reform Board, district collectors, *taluk tahsildar*s, village committees and land tribunals.

Land Reforms: The Subtleties

The reforms were not a mere administrative event but a political one with the scope to radically transform the socio-economic structure of the state. A solid

---

[7] Government of Kerala, *Report of the Task Force on Land Reforms and Agrarian Institutions* (Trivandrum: State Planning Board, 1997).

[8] Ronald Herring, 'Embedded Particularism: India's Failed Developmental State', in *The Developmental State*, ed. Meredith Woo-Cumings, 306–34 (Ithaca, NY: Cornell University Press, 1999).

historic bond between the political struggles of the princely era and effective
legislation was crucial in implementing land reforms.

The land reforms have stimulated academic debates and sharpened
political positions regarding their fairness, social and economic consequences,
and the structural changes they brought in. Early assessments focused on
inequality. Herring offered a complex interpretation of the reforms.[9] He said
it was a mistake to assume that all tenants were similar and benefited from
the reforms equally. A 1976 survey classified households into landlords, rich
peasants, middle peasants, poor peasants and mixed class. The mixed class
needed special attention as they neither qualified as peasants nor as landlords.
Herring argued that ambiguous and heterogeneous class structure had led to
more limited gains for the landless labourers and some benefits for the rich
peasants.

Later assessments shifted to productivity. Pulapre Balakrishnan says
that the land reform was a failure. It could 'only distribute the land' rather
than increase productivity.[10] By stressing the food security crises (Chapter 3),
Balakrishnan asks the government of the state to revise its anti-tenancy law
to return the redistributed land if it is not being cultivated.

The reform laws provoked massive evasive measures by the landlords,
who anticipated land reforms with communists coming to power. There
was a consistent confusion over whom the land reforms exclusively aimed
at. Although determined to protect landless labourers, the reforms also
accommodated the interests of poor and middle-class peasants. Seen by some
as an attempt to bring proletarian empowerment, the reforms were reluctant
to attack small landholders. The implementation setup often followed the
rule book closely, to the detriment of an understanding of the realities of the
area.

Subsequent reforms benefited the tenants but put the Dalits and Adivasis
at a further disadvantage. By conferring tenant status to settler farmers who
had either encroached on or acquired tribal lands, the act of 1969 marginalised
the Adivasis further, as most did not possess legal documentary evidence
to prove their entitlement.[11] Much later, the Kerala Restriction on Transfer

---

[9] Ronald J. Herring, *Land to the Tiller: The Political Economy of Agrarian Reform in
    South Asia* (Delhi: Oxford University Press, 1983).
[10] Pulapre Balakrishnan, 'Imagining an Economy of Plenty in Kerala', *Economic and
    Political Weekly* 43, no. 20 (2008): 14–16.
[11] Ravi Raman, 'Breaking New Ground'.

and Restoration of Lands to Scheduled Tribes, 1999, again privileged the settled farmers and was vehemently opposed by the Adivasi communities. This was the first time in the history of the Adivasi movements in the state that they demanded the right to land for the landless rather than solely the restoration of alienated land. The mode of protests was powerful, where they portrayed their culture and disseminated the message of solidarity and peace. It signalled that the Adivasis were speaking for themselves, rejecting political patronisation. The major achievement of the struggle was that they were able to break free of the limited spectrum of restoration and create a new framework under which they could demand recognition of continuous possession. V. S. Achuthanandan, who later became the chief minister, took a stand against the land grabbing of corporate plantations. During his tenure between 2006 and 2011, a programme named 'Operation Munnar' was initiated which aimed at taking back the land grabbed by the plantations. Not less than 1,280 acres of land owned by the Kannan Devan Hills was seized by the government. Another 16,000 acres of land was identified, on which no other actions have been taken yet. Despite these movements, land ownership remained highly unequal in the state. According to the National Sample Survey report (2003), 65 per cent of the Scheduled Tribes face absolute landlessness. The corresponding figure for Scheduled Castes and Other Backward Classes was 24 per cent.

By the early 1980s, there had begun a drastic change in the land market with the inflow of remittances. Since then, land has steadily become more of a means of exchange and speculation and less of a means of production. There was a decline in the interest in growing food crops, and a change started in the cropping pattern. This change resulted in the state's increased food dependency on neighbouring states (Chapter 3). Urbanisation and urban construction boom imposed new pressures on the land market and further alienated marginalised communities.

Keeping in step with these changes and not ready to give up on the mission to create a just society, the focus of the government shifted from land distribution towards infrastructural help. In 2016, when the communists led by Pinarayi Vijayan came back to power, the government introduced the Livelihood Inclusion Financial Empowerment (LIFE) Mission. The mission's target was to provide safe housing to 430,000 households within five years. The beneficiaries would be provided with housing and social services, including primary healthcare, senior support, skill development and provision for financial services inclusion. Priority was given to the coastal population, plantation workers and those who stayed in temporary shelters on government lands. The left government has not dropped the idea of distributing land to landless Adivasis and Dalits. There appears to be progress in providing land to the landless, in addition to taking steps to empower the marginalised outside of land resources. This was also one of the factors that brought back the Pinarayi government for a second term.[12]

Labour

In 1958, for the first time in India the communist government (1957–59) introduced the Kerala Minimum Wage Rules. Currently, Kerala workers receive the highest wage rate in India, which is nearly twice the average wage rate. Kerala was also the first state to establish welfare fund boards for its workers beginning with the Toddy Tappers Welfare Fund board in 1969. It was the same year that the Kerala Dinesh Beedi Workers Cooperative Society was also formed.

It was a result of the cooperative and welfare fund board experiments that many cooperatives were formed in the state and a variety of welfare boards across sectors were formed. The cooperative sector itself diversified. This was further strengthened by amalgamation of district cooperative banks into the Kerala Bank in 2019.

The Minimum Wages Advisory Board holds tripartite meetings to determine the minimum wages for 84 sectors. Kerala Welfare Fund Act, 1975, was a significant legislative step. The laws were constantly updated and enhanced, such as with the Minimum Wage Act (Kerala Amendment), 2017, the Maternity Benefit (Amendment) Act, 2017, and the Industrial Dispute (Kerala Amendment) Act, 2017.

Kerala also undertook significant steps, again possibly the first among Indian states, to ensure welfare of inter-state migrants. The left government established an agency named the Non-Resident Keralites Affairs (NORKA),[13] aimed at delivering welfare for the migrants. The government took measures to reintegrate the returning migrants who also come under attractive pension schemes, under the aegis of NORKA roots. This commitment towards the

---

[12] Ravi Raman, 'The Opposition "Emocracy" Exposed'.

[13] For more details, Kerala State Planning Board, *Kerala Human Development Report* (2021) (Thiruvananthapuram: Government of Kerala, 2021), 242–252.

migrant workers was taken further with the setting up of the Loka Kerala Sabha which act as a platform for the Malayali diaspora community, utilising the expertise of the non-resident Keralites for the development of the state, while formulating policies which will benefit them.

Education

The first communist government had a radical education policy favouring the nationalisation of education. From long before the formation of the state, Christian churches and caste organisations such as the Shree Narayana Dharma Paripalana Sangham (SNDP), Muslim Education Society (MES) and Nair Service Society (NSS) had made their presence felt in schools and colleges in the state. In 1956, of the about 10,000 schools, a little over 2,000 were government schools. The rest were either government-aided or private unaided schools. Private investment played a critical role in improving literacy levels, and communities competed to set up schools for the benefit of their members. Private education had its problems. It could exclude students and certainly prioritise members of preferred communities. The teachers were often placed on an inferior plane with no occupational assurance and always at risk of dismissal.

Six days following his swearing in as a Minister of Education of the first communist government, Joseph Mundasery declared his intention to legislate on governing the operation of the aided schools. The Education Bill of 1957 announced a phased nationalisation of the entire system, standardisation of salaries and elimination of all forms of discrimination. All the institutions of collegiate education would come under the guidance and control of the proposed Kerala University (formerly Travancore University). Technical education received a new emphasis. The government also expressed concerns over regional inequality and opened thirty high schools in the Malabar area alone in 1957–58. The Education Bill invited the fury of private management and caste organisations. Amidst violent protests from various private agencies and with 310 amendments, the bill could finally be passed in September 1957 but was not implemented as the government was dismissed in 1959.

Subsequently, all governments maintained their commitment to primary education and accelerated the growth of the infrastructure. The combined public–private-community efforts helped advance the educational sector even as the population of children was growing rapidly with the demographic transition. In 1988, the central government formed the National Literacy Mission to make all individuals between the ages of 15 and 35 literate. The Kerala Association for Nonformal Education and Development (KANFED), which coordinated the literacy activities, aimed at creating a fully literate *panchayat*. In 1989, the Kerala Shastra Sahitya Parishad (KSSP) also formulated a literacy campaign. These campaigns delivered a further boost to literacy. In 1990, Ernakulam became the first fully literate district in the country. Chief Minister E. K. Nayanar declared that the whole state would become fully literate in a year. Following a survey to identify the still non-literates, hundreds of thousands of volunteers worked to meet that commitment. On 8 April 1991, Kerala became India's first fully literate state. In 2022, the literacy rate was 96.2 per cent, against 77.7 per cent in all of India. The strength of the final push had owed to the agencies that had already existed in the state in the service of education, and not just government effort.

Health

When the state was created in 1956, it had to deal with insufficient food availability, poor nutrition and inequitable regional growth. As in education, post-1956 health advancements also benefited from past contributions. Historically, while Travancore and Cochin had experienced significant progress, Malabar had lagged. The first elected communist government wanted to bridge this regional disparity and attempted to bring an inclusive and well-networked public healthcare system. The Thiruvananthapuram Medical College (TMC), the oldest medical college in south India, was inaugurated in 1951. The Government Medical College Hospital appeared on the same campus three years later. The Travancore state had opened its first significant dispensary in Thiruvananthapuram in 1914. It expanded to the first Women and Children Hospital, where Mary Punnen Lukose, an English-trained gynaecologist, became the nation's first woman surgeon-general.

Malabar had seen little development, comparatively speaking. The first communist government proposed to set up a Headquarters Hospital in each district, which would be responsible for the supply of medicine and hospital equipment. In May 1957, the government set up the Kozhikode Medical College and discussed the idea of travelling medical units. The Public Health Department became active in the supply of protected water to congested urban areas.

No matter which party ruled, the state continued to significantly increase the size of its public health facilities between 1961 and 1986. Government hospital beds expanded from roughly 13,000 in 1960 to 21,000 in 1970, 29,000 in 1980 and 36,000 in 1996. After that, it declined significantly. From the 1980s, the drive started to slow, whereas the private health sector gradually emerged as the state's main healthcare supplier. Private providers of services had always been present. The new trend, fed by remittances, was the establishment of hospitals, nursing homes and specialist treatment units. Between 1986 and 1996, the number of beds in government institutions increased from 36,000 to 38,000, while the number in private institutions increased from 49,000 to 67,500. The private sector outperformed the public on cutting-edge diagnostic and therapeutic techniques, drawing visitors from other states.

The latest intervention by the left government, the Clinical Establishment Bill, 2018, expects to alter how the commercial health industry operates. According to surveys, marginalised social groups still lack access to proper healthcare services, and this is especially true for indigenous people and fishermen. Regional disparities remain, with Malabar lagging behind Travancore in terms of access to better and more services. An inverse relationship exists between socioeconomic status and morbidity. The ageing of the population and the massive influx of migrants from other states pose new challenges. The bill addresses some of these trends.

Public Distribution of Food

Concerning food, the deficit was of the order of 50 per cent when the state was formed. The state had the largest food deficit in India and depended on the centre or the proximate surplus states such as Andhra Pradesh and Tamil Nadu. The food situation was not so bad in the early nineteenth century but worsened during it. For instance, Travancore was once a net exporter of its staple food, rice, but had become a net importer by the last quarter of the nineteenth century.[14] Despite Malabar being the second-largest producer of rice in the Madras Presidency, next only to Thanjavur, it also became a net importer of paddy from the mid-nineteenth century. In both provinces, the

[14] T. K. Velu Pillai, *The Travancore State Manual* (4 vols.), vol. 3 (Trivandrum: Government Press, 1940), 90.

fall in rice production was compensated for only by increased rice imports from Burma (Myanmar). Behind the relative food shortage, population growth played a role. Besides, the rapid commercialisation of agriculture had a bias towards cash crops, which led to a decrease in the area under food crops.

During World War II, food shortages became acute in many parts of India. Peasants in Malabar and industrial workers in Travancore struggled against the landlords and employers who kept large quantities of rice in their private warehouses. The agitation went to the extent of confiscating the godowns and distributing the rice and paddy to the poor by forming producers and consumers co-operatives in the early 1940s. Rationing was informally introduced by the mid-1940s in various parts of the state. The newly formed state had to wait until 1965 for the formal functioning of the rationing system in the state.

Partly driven by persistent regional inequality, successive governments maintained their commitment to food security via public distribution. The National Food Security Act (NFSA), 2013, by the Government of India was a significant step taken to address the issue of food security. When the communist-led coalition formed a government in 2016, implementing NFSA was a top priority. In 2011–12, 53 per cent of the rural population and 50 per cent of the urban population were brought under the act. Via these means, and the Midday Meal Scheme and the Integrated Child Development Scheme (ICDS), the NFSA, 2013, was instrumentalised effectively.

Democracy and Decentralisation

The first communist government introduced the Kerala Panchayat Bill in 1958, knowing well that the decentralisation practiced under the President's Rule in Travancore–Cochin was inadequate to bridge the gulf between the bureaucracy and the people. It was also aware that the 'evils of the system' that had been handed over to them by the British and the princely rulers demanded drastic reforms. As the ministry collapsed, the bill lapsed. In 1960, Pattom Thanu Pillai successfully implemented the Kerala Panchayat Bill, which recommended the division of local bodies for better and more efficient administration. The same Praja Socialist–led government also consecutively implemented the Kerala Municipal Bill and the Kerala

Municipal Corporation Bill in 1960 and 1961. All these bills had the same idea: bringing the government closer to the people.

There were several attempts to introduce local self-government in the 1960s without much success due to political disruptions and discontinuities. Only in 1994 could the Congress-led K. Karunakaran ministry implement the Kerala Panchayat Raj Bill and Kerala Municipality Bill. The Panchayat Raj Bill enacted a three-tier local self-government system and invested special powers in these institutions. Here, local administrative bodies acted as the centres of welfare policies through which people were exposed to the functioning of the state. This has smoothened the functioning of *panchayats* and bridged the distance between the government and the people to a large extent. Since 1995, the three-tier local government institutions (*grama*, block and district *panchayats*) have been implementing development plans.[15] Chapter 6 discusses the outcomes of the decentralisation move in more detail, though many essential details remain unavailable.

Among other initiatives on empowerment, the left-dominated social and scientific group, Kerala Shastra Sahitya Parishad (KSSP), has been at the forefront of the People's Planning Movement, and they have actively demanded the use of modern technology and science in bridging the gap between the state and the people. Their involvement in the movement was also a continuation of their role in various other campaigns, including the literacy movement. Nevertheless, the performance of these plans has been generally unsatisfactory. as they lost momentum after the initial years.

Kudumbashree, a community network of over 4.3 million units, played a crucial role in eradicating poverty and empowering women. Founded in 1996 as part of the People's Plan Campaign, again by the left government, it promotes microenterprises and innovative programmes under the local self-government. Originally begun as a poverty eradication programme, the Kudumbashree mission has expanded its activities by setting up neighbourhood groups (NHGs) and women community networks, thereby helping the state in reducing the multiple dimensions of poverty. The role played by Kudumbashree whenever the state was in crisis, such as the 2018–19 floods and the Covid-19 pandemic, was significant.

The achievements in democratic decentralisation often became known as the 'New Kerala Model'. It implies two things: the building up of democratic

---

[15] R. G. Sreelekha, 'Democracy and Development at the Grassroots People's Planning in Vithura Panchayat – A Case Study' (PhD Dissertation, University of Kerala, 2014).

institutions at the local level and the devolution of plan funds to local village *panchayat*s. The state would support the local institutions; they would also be supported by expert knowledge. This was also a part of the all-India project of the Congress government. More than that, it came out as part of a political campaign by the left forces when they were in opposition. This also helped them win the election in 1996. The role played by the left parties and associations, such as the KSSP, was critical in making decentralisation of power an all-encompassing agenda. They helped in resource mapping, integrated local institutions with the larger civil society, and implemented local development in terms of roads and water projects.

Conclusion

Lest this chapter seems like a manifesto for the communist parties in the state, it is necessary to say why we decided to write this chapter. Communism as an ideological movement has significantly declined with the resurgence of global capitalism since the 1990s. So have communist parties contesting democratic elections worldwide. Kerala is an exception to that norm. And it is an exception for a reason. The left movement was built around a campaign to redress inequality. From the start, the movement's leaders understood that inequality in this part of India was not based on class alone but on class mixed up with specific local forms of caste-based discrimination and deprivation. However, they did not always agree on what the response should be. That agenda made the Communist Party in the state different from its counterparts elsewhere. The distinctive face of the movement was one reason behind its endurance.

In practice, the left had one dominant response to inequality, land reform, which delivered some equality but caused agricultural decline and did not alter much the conditions of parts of the population with tenuous rights to agricultural land. While pursuing that programme, the old left also unnecessarily damaged the state's attraction to private investors.

The land reform agenda had become dangerously obsolete by the 1980s. The state and its left politics might face a severe crisis. But savings and investments started to rise, first via the migration–remittance route and later via business growth. These new trends and reforms in the fiscal system India-wide improved public finances. And the state could avoid continued spending on health and education because private investment surged in both fields. Labour export and remittances – the market – saved the Kerala Model. The reforms and investments in health and education resulted in the creation of skilled labour. This also had an impact on the demographic transition in the state (see Chapter 6). The left could now afford to shift focus to other forms of inequality and, increasingly, infrastructure and environment. This quiet reinvention and playing the market was a second reason for the left's endurance in the state.

What about the other parties? A strong emphasis on inequality marked the left out in the political landscape of Kerala. This was their distinctive imprint upon the state's long-term development pathway. On sustaining the state's head start in primary education and healthcare, there was little difference across the political spectrum and little change in direction when governments changed. No thanks to any particular political party, committed expenditures on these heads (which mostly go to pay for salaries) dominated the budget and still do. Undoubtedly, these institutions made for much greater accessibility to primary education and basic healthcare than in almost any other state of India – the hallmarks of the Kerala Model – but also contributed to the pursuit of equality.

Our final topic is the environment, a business asset (Chapter 4) but a vulnerable one.

8

Geography

An Asset or a Challenge?

The state's climate is unique among Indian states. Following the Köppen–Geiger classification of climatic regions of the world, over two-thirds of the land in India is tropical savanna, desert or semi-arid. Most of Kerala is monsoonal or highland tropics. The difference is this. The average summer temperature in the former regions can reach levels high enough to dry up surface water. The monsoon rains relieve that aridity, but only for a few months in a year. That dual condition makes water storage and recycling a fundamental precondition for economic growth. It elevates the risk of droughts and diseases from seasonal or periodic acute water shortages. Kerala, by contrast, does not get as fierce a summer as the other areas of India and receives a lot more rainfall. That dual condition implies a natural immunity from seasonal food and water scarcity and a low disease risk.

With its extraordinary biodiversity, this is a vast storehouse for natural resources. The state has a surface area of 38,855 square kilometres and is bounded by the Arabian Sea to the west and the Western Ghats to the east. The eastern highlands, the central midlands and the western lowlands, with 580 kilometres of coastline, can access a wealth of ocean resources and means of subsistence for their fisherfolk and the general populace. Compared with semi-arid India, the benign environment largely explains the head start in life expectancy (Chapters 1 and 6). Further, nature provides industrial resources that cannot be found elsewhere. The highlands have the ideal climate for growing coffee, tea and spices. Low hills are often planted with rubber. The seaboard traded with West Asia for centuries. The state's Gulf connection, thus, had a prehistory. A large tourism business has developed by selling nature.

On the other hand, recent experience shows that climate change and overdevelopment can jointly raise the risk of disasters. In the first three weeks of August 2018, Kerala received 164 per cent of the average rainfall for that time of the year. The following floods were devastating, comparable only to a similar event in 1924. In 2019, extreme weather repeated, now causing landslides. Mining and quarrying, frequent blasting and unscientific changes in land use patterns affected the highland ecology. The highlands also house no fewer than 39 dams and reservoirs, most of which were built for irrigation and hydroelectric power generation, but some also changed the landscape.

Over the long run, forces acting upon the natural environment have shifted. In the nineteenth century, logging and plantations caused significant deforestation. In the middle decades of the twentieth century, large factories were established in the state as part of the public-sector-led industrialisation drive. These factories utilised their natural resources. Some of these, from rayon to cement to heavy chemicals, caused local pollution of water and air. Possibly the most potent force of change has been private construction since the end of the twentieth century, fed first by Gulf money and later by rising average incomes. At first, these were private dwelling places, but, more recently, most of the new construction served service-sector business enterprises such as hotels, schools and hospitals. Given the state's conventional settlement pattern, these houses were spread out over a large area. In areas with high flooding and landslide risk, the incidence of disaster damage has risen.

These initial remarks suggest the outline of a chronological narrative of the environment–economy interaction in the state since 1956. The rest of the chapter is organised around these three themes, separated in time.

Deforestation and Industrial Pollution

From the nineteenth century, observers of the plantations in the highlands noticed the close connection between monoculture plantations and a host of distortions, such as the drying up of streams, flooding and soil erosion. By the middle of the nineteenth century, European enterprises in the high and midlands of Travancore and Malabar, growing coffee, tea and later rubber, destroyed forests. An experienced British planter, W. S. S. Mackay, said, '[T]he early planters were sometimes careless in their attitude to preservation, but in those days the evergreen jungles were so vast that few contemplated their appreciable reduction.'[1] Other colonial-era projects that caused extensive change in land use and conversion of forests into arable land were the few large dams that emerged, like the Mullaperiyar dam, which involved leasing out forest lands and the destruction of fauna such as ibex, deer, bison, wild boar, panther, tiger and elephants.

If these destructions were localised and mainly concentrated in the highland estates, similar damages caused by the construction of dozens of hydroelectric-cum-irrigation projects after the formation of the state involved a much larger extent of land than what the estates commanded, and often a more radical alteration of the landscape.

By the 1970s, the need for a balanced eco-development framework became apparent, and a green movement emerged in the state. The opposition to big dams came to a head in the campaign against the Silent Valley multipurpose dam project that began in the late 1970s. Silent Valley is a deep forest cover located at the northeast corner of Palakkad district, with an area of 8,952 hectares in the southernmost part of the Western Ghats. The river Kunti originates from Silent Valley and is a major waterway that flows through the tropical evergreen forests and mountain terrain. One of India's rare and unpenetrated rain forests, Silent Valley is known for its rare flora and fauna and the region's delicate ecosystem. In 1975, the Planning Commission permitted the establishment of an arch dam across Kunti. The Save Silent Valley campaign forced the state to withdraw from the project. The movement played a vital role in stressing the environmental cost of development projects. It showed the possibility of broad agreement among scientists, technologists, bureaucrats, environmentalists and ordinary people on the conservation and preservation of biodiversity.

Some pre-independence industrial factories (spinning mills in Kollam [Quilon], coir in Alapuzha, a paper mill in Punalur and others) also had adverse environmental consequences – but not quite on the scale that the post-independence large factories did. The Fertilizer and Chemical Travancore Limited (FACT), C. P. Ramaswamy Iyer's favourite (Chapter 4), was formed in 1944. After 1947, Travancore Cochin Chemicals Limited, Hindustan Insecticides Limited and the Indian Rare Earth Limited (IRE) were formed. All polluted air and water. With rare earths, residents gained

---

[1] Cited in K. Ravi Raman, *Global Capital and Peripheral Labour: The History and Political Economy of Plantation Workers in India* (Abingdon: Routledge, 2010), 41.

a lot from the subsequent growth of allied businesses in the area but also suffered serious water pollution.

Private enterprises such as Hindalco and Bombay Suburban Electric Supply Kerala Power Limited (BKPL) also had some role. In 1954, Hindustan Insecticides Limited, a central government enterprise, was launched. The toxicities that were generated made water unusable and species survival difficult. In 2004, the endosulfan plant of Hindustan Insecticides Limited emitted toxic gases into the atmosphere. The emission of hazardous gases in the atmosphere and the discharge of chemical and toxic elements and factory waste in Periyar had posed severe health threats to local residents. Vembanad lake also suffered.

The rayon factory closed due to labour disputes and the depletion of the resource base. Among the more recent cases of managed industrialisation, in 2001, the government invited Hindustan Beverages to set up a Coca-Cola factory in Palakkad. The fate of the industry was no different from the rayon case. It damaged local livelihoods by polluting the local water resources and shut down after a series of protests by environmentalists in the state.[2]

Land Use

The state underwent significant changes in its land use pattern. First of all, there was a large increase (168 per cent from 1970 to 2015) in operational holdings, while the total area under agricultural operations declined by 13 per cent. In the earlier half of this timespan, the area operated increased, but the subdivision of holdings happened because of the division of family land shares from generation to generation. The population was then growing relatively fast. Between 1990 and 2016, the area shrank, while subdivisions continued, mainly because of land conversion to commercial uses and urban homes. Thus, marginal holdings dominated agriculture.

This process did not happen uniformly in all districts. In the 2010s, in Wayanad, Thrissur, Kozhikode, Malappuram and Kannur, lands previously used for mixed crops and those put aside as fallow were converted to

---

[2] K. Ravi Raman, 'Corporate Violence, Legal Nuances and Political Ecology: Cola War in Plachimada', *Economic and Political Weekly* 40, no. 25 (2005): 2481–86; K. Ravi Raman, 'Transverse Solidarity: Water, Power and Resistance', *Review of Radical Political Economics* 42, no. 2 (2010): 251–68.

agricultural lands. Much of the fallow was converted into built-up lands. In the highlands, the area under plantations increased in the 2010s, whereas plantations were shrinking in the 1980s. Capitalism and improvements in standards of living in recent years have been the main drivers behind these changes. Reduced economic viability of agriculture, labour shortages and population pressure on land are the major drivers behind the transformation of paddy fields to other land uses.[3]

Land used for commercial purposes has grown by 32 per cent since about 2010. Between 1980 and 2010, the built-up commercial area increased more than tenfold, pointing to the deep structural shift away from agriculture towards services. A new form of industrialisation set in (Chapter 4). There has been a sharp growth in industrial built-ups since the 2000s. Ernakulum contributed almost one-third of this rise. Data for several districts are unavailable, but impressions suggest that most experienced a growth of small- and medium-scale industry.

Residential land usage increased more than eleven times between 1980 and 2020. Although there was a reduction in residential land between 2000 and 2010, it was negligible and might have been a consequence of the recession at the end of the 2000s. Between 2010 and 2021, residential land use increased by four times. All districts, especially Palakkad, Wayanad, Kozhikode, Malappuram and Kannur, contributed generously to the increase in residential built-ups.

The biggest loser in the process was paddy cultivation. Paddy lands increased in 1980–2000 but fell after that, reducing almost by half in the last two decades. The sharp decline in paddy production increased the state's dependence on food from neighbouring states and the central pool and increased the vulnerability of the paddy ecosystem. Apart from providing food security and rural employment, the rice ecosystem also includes the preservation of biodiversity, land conservation and renewable natural resources. As elsewhere in Asia, the recent urbanisation, commercialisation

---

[3] M. Jose and M. Padmanabhan, 'Dynamics of Agricultural Land Use Change in Kerala: A Policy and Social-ecological Perspective', *International Journal of Agricultural Sustainability* 14, no. 3 (2016): 307–24; G. Prasad and M. V. Ramesh, 'Spatio-temporal Analysis of Land Use/Land Cover Changes in an Ecologically Fragile Area—Alappuzha District, Southern Kerala, India', *Natural Resources Research* 28, Supplement 1 (2019): 31–42.

and conversion of paddy fields threaten the rice-based ecosystems in the state.

The relationship between land use change, built-up area expansion and urbanisation can be explored by taking a few case studies. In the case of Alappuzha, for instance, a major transformation has been recorded in land use and urbanisation. The area under mixed vegetation has increased marginally since 2000. The rise in mixed vegetation – plants, trees (such as coconut or plantain), herbs and other crops – reflects an increase in domestic use on residential premises and the growth of homestead lands. The area under paddy fields has reduced, especially in the southern and northern parts of the district, while cultivation continues only in the Kuttanad area. Population growth was around 27 per cent, leading to a growth in the built-up area. The area of uncultivated land reduced sharply. The rapid expansion of built-up areas happened because of urbanisation, rural-to-urban migration, particularly towards district centres, and the development of tourism infrastructure around Vembanad lake. In the southern part of the district, socio-economic development improvements also substantially increased built-up land. The development threatened the delicate environmental balance by overusing natural resources and worsening waste management issues.

Forests and forest plantations have not undergone such drastic changes in the last forty years. However, the abovementioned trends put pressure upon forest-dependent communities that did not have secure private property rights. The encroachment of the Mathikettan Mala, situated within the Cardamom Hill Reserve Area, is an example of the troubled management of the balance between marginalised groups and forest conservation. Mathikettan Mala is an evergreen forest located in Idukki. The forest provides a habitat to the species present there, of which 70 per cent are endemic. This ecologically fragile forest land is crucial in regulating climatic conditions and preserving the area's sensitive and rich biodiversity. In 2001, large-scale land encroachment and deforestation was reported in Mathikettan. This was not a sudden incident; it had been going on since 1996. An order issued in 2001 stating that the Mathikettan Mala land would be distributed among the landless tribal communities escalated encroachment. The settlers cleared the fragile forest land. Such a large-scale encroachment and deforestation would not have been possible without the tacit help of forest officers and assistance from bureaucratic agencies. There were other incidents like this one, sometimes aided by the land mafia in the state.

Nelliyambathi, a green belt of the Parambikulam wildlife sanctuary, has
been subjected to illegal encroachment, logging and mining since at least the
1990s. Like in the case of Mathikettan Mala, the deforestation was carried
out with a tacit agreement between the perpetrators and officers. Those
affected were mobilised, mostly democratically, but often through violent
means. As in the previous case, the rights and livelihoods of the marginalised
Adivasi and Dalit communities were again compromised.[4]

Urbanisation

The urban population in the state has increased from 13.5 per cent to 48
per cent in fifty years (1961–2011). The acceleration started in the 1980s.
According to the 2011 census, among the major Indian states, Kerala recorded
the highest urbanisation rate. The high urbanisation rate is characterised by
the shift in the workforce from the agriculture sector to the tertiary sector.
Population projection reports say that by the end of the 2030s, nearly 90 per
cent of the population will be urban.

The dynamics of urbanisation have been unique. Most people in the
state live in clusters of houses that are hard to classify as a town or a village.
Urbanisation is induced and characterised by the transformation of clusters
as they acquire urban characteristics (more commercial spaces and public
and private services, for one thing) rather than rural–urban migration.

Urban density reflects this change well. According to the census
definition of urban, one of the indicators is to have a minimum density of
400 persons per square kilometre. The state has had an average population
density of more than 400 persons per square kilometre since its formation
in 1956. In the last forty years, the general population density increased
by almost 90 per cent, while the change in urban density was only 15 per
cent. This shows that not much population was added to the existing urban
areas. Instead, settlements were spread and reclassified as the population
concentrated. The largest towns, including Kochi, Thiruvananthapuram and
Kozhikode, did not become significantly more extensive, whereas the fringes

---

[4] K. Ravi Raman, 'Subaltern Modernity: Kerala, The Eastern Theatre of Resistance in
The Global South', *Sociology: British Association of Sociology* 51, no. 1 (2017): 91–110;
K. Ravi Raman, *Political Ecospatiality: Protests and Politics in Kerala* (Cambridge:
Cambridge University Press, forthcoming).

of these urban centres experienced a higher rate of density change. The spatial characteristics of urbanisation exhibited an organic way of growth, often referred to as ribbon development, with highly densified development along the transport corridors and leaving utilised pockets in the interiors.[5] The major urban settlements came up along the transportation corridors. Within the core city, it is difficult to manage the density pattern due to the small size of land holdings and the larger number of landowners. In the periphery regions, the intensity of development is comparatively high on land adjoining the roads.

Dispersed settlements and low-density urbanisation made developing infrastructure such as transportation, water supply, sewerage and solid waste management a massive challenge. A shortage of land for affordable housing and immigration resulted in squatter settlements in environmentally sensitive zones. These settlements were severely affected by the floods and landslides during the monsoon season in 2018 and again in 2019.

Because of the settlement pattern, conventionally, the government framed local development policies without making a strict distinction between the rural and the urban. The planning and development at the local level follow an annual planning framework. The thrust has been on local self-government, which is less challenging than in most Indian states because the capacity of the local units is not so variable from one another. In the process, a functional spatial planning system remains undeveloped, and land development regulations are not very effective. In terms of urbanisation, which is taking place fast, the state is neither spatially polarised nor unbalanced between core and semi-peripheries, a rural–urban continuum is the fundamental feature, with urban amenities available throughout the state.

Among the consequences of the unchecked rise in commercial and residential land use, the foremost is elevated disaster risk.

Disaster Risk

Studies assessing the role of land use changes in the 2020 floods highlighted how changes in the green cover dynamics altered hydrology and enhanced

---

[5] Government of Kerala, *Kerala State Urbanisation Report* (Thiruvananthapuram: Local Self Government Department, 2012).

the risks of floods and landslides.[6] In 1985–2018, there was a slight reduction in barren or sparsely vegetated areas. In 2005–18, evergreen forests showed a slight increase. However, there was a significant decrease in mixed forest cover and a rise in dwellings. Shrubland and grasslands fell. These changes made the risk of flooding more extensive. The discharge, inundation area and flood surface height all changed, possibly because of land use changes.

The Kerala State Disaster Management Plan 2016 identifies the state as a multi-hazard-prone region. Vulnerability comes from landslides, floods, cyclones, storm surges and sea erosion. Disasters caused substantial loss of human lives and property, and economic and social disruption. Further, the erosion along the 590-kilometre coastline created major damage to coastal habitats and communities. The Kerala State Biodiversity Board conducted a rapid assessment to gauge the impact of floods on biodiversity. This assessment revealed that a total of 771 different landscapes, encompassing riverine, forest, plantations and agricultural fields, were adversely affected. The Building Regulatory Capacity Assessment report of the World Bank reveals that land use change in the state has been cited as one of the factors contributing to frequent disasters (landslides and floods) in the state.

The floods and landslides of 2018 and 2019 led to a series of reassessments, both on the extent of the risk and on the causes.[7] These said that unregulated growth of residential areas along riverbanks and water bodies, deforestation in the upper catchments and the narrowing of floodplains contributed to increased flood risks. Also, insufficient storm water drainage systems and the accumulation of silt in minor storage ponds and floodplains in urban

---

[6] S. L. Kuriakose, G. Sankar and C. Muraleedharan, 'History of Landslide Susceptibility and a Chorology of Landslide-Prone Areas in The Western Ghats of Kerala, India', *Environmental Geology* 57, no. 7 (2019): 1553–68; Government of Kerala and UNDP, *Post Disaster Needs Assessment: Floods and Landslides* (Thiruvananthapuram: Government of Kerala, 2019).

[7] K. Ravi Raman, 'Ecospatiality: Transforming Kerala's Post-flood Riskscapes', *Cambridge Journal of Regions, Economy and Society* 13, no. 2 (2020): 319–41. See also K. P. Sudheer, M. Bhallamudi, B. Narasimhan, J. Thomas, V. M. Bindhu, V. K. Vema and C. Kurian, 'Role of Dams on the Floods of August 2018 in Periyar River Basin, Kerala', *Current Science* 116, no. 5 (2019): 780–94; Kerala State Council for Science, Technology and Environment (KSCSTE), *Committee to Examine the Causes of Repeated Extreme Heavy Rainfall Events, Subsequent Floods and Landslides and to Recommend Appropriate Policy Responses* (Thiruvananthapuram: Government of Kerala, 2019).

and sprawling areas were potentially damaging. Floodwater washed away houses built in the floodplains of active rivers, and drainage culverts along roads were not appropriately positioned to manage water flow effectively. As the environmental risks were by and large non-neutral, it was the poor and marginalised who had to bear the major brunt. This necessitates a policy shift in risk transfer mechanisms in the state.[8]

Conclusion

To a great extent, the economic pathway was shaped by resources – natural resources, landscape as a resource for tourism, and labour export. Its record of high levels of human development may have contributed to using these assets but in no direct or fundamental way. Markets ruled throughout. By contrast with other states, population growth, industrial effluents and agricultural commercialisation were relatively less concerning causal variables of environmental change. But construction was another matter. The state's pathway of economic change intrinsically created some vulnerabilities. For example, tourism might lead to construction in remote highland areas, blocking natural runoff. In the last twenty years, that pathway has delivered such a rapid rise in living standards as to add to these vulnerabilities. Remittances did this first via a private dwelling construction boom and later via the building of commercial spaces. These risks became mainstream topics in development policymaking only after the acute disasters of 2018–19.

Kerala's urbanisation is distinct from the counterpart process in the rest of India. It involves the emergence of a denser rural–urban continuum where the rural can hardly be distinguished from the urban, except for a few characteristics. If certain pockets in the high ranges are excluded, villages isolated from the urban do not exist in Kerala. This means that as livelihoods and settlements change, huge investments in urban infrastructure are needed. This has indeed been a major focus of policy in the state in recent years.

We have concluded the theme-wise narrative account. The last chapter restates and stresses the key lessons and uses these to speculate on the state's economic future.

---

[8] Government of Kerala, *Report of the Committee on Risk Transfer Mechanism for Disaster Risk Financing* (Thiruvananthapuram: Government of Kerala, 2021).

9

Conclusion

Kerala Is Different ... Not the Way You Think

The book began with a one-liner – 'Kerala is different'. The series to which this book belongs emerged from the intuition that every state in India 'is different'. Kerala was not more different than Tamil Nadu, Gujarat or West Bengal. Geography and resource endowments, social conditions such as patterns of inequality, politics and markets were significantly dissimilar between the larger Indian states, and sometimes between regions within these states. Scholars doing development or history have not explored the differences enough.

And yet that shallow slogan has had an unparalleled impact on development discourse in the late twentieth century. Why has this one state drawn so much attention in the development scholarship? Because of a misreading of its economic history, the book argues.

As we mentioned in the introduction, the state's economic trajectory can be summed up, if crudely, with a chart with three lines, one measuring economic growth and the other two education and life expectancy. The state's position relative to India fell with the social indices but dramatically improved with economic growth. A preoccupation with social development lacks a strong justification, at least for economic historians of the state. The more challenging task for us was explaining the economic growth divergence with reference to prehistory and the state's geography.

The misreading emerged in the 1980s through an overstatement of human development performance. Many scholars inferred that the state's political ideology was more enlightened and developmental than that of other Indian provinces and that the state government's heart was in the right place. Whether due to the communist movement or Travancore and Cochin's princely heritage, the governments prioritised poor people's access to primary education and healthcare. Others further claimed that the state showed the world that economic growth was not needed for development.

This reading is not wrong. But, historically speaking, it is a naïve reading. It is naïve for three reasons. First, suppose Kerala was ahead of India in the 1950s and 1960s. In that case, a story of enlightened government does not make much sense because governments were relatively small then, and many factors besides the government were at work behind the initial advances in education and health. To the extent the government was active, it was because of higher fiscal capacity; the princely states could extract more taxes thanks to a globally connected capitalism utilising the abundance of natural resources. Second, as demographers have shown, the state's unusual human development record also owed to its benign environment, whereas most of India struggled against aridity and uncertain rainfall. These two arguments question the hyping of government at a neglect of markets and resource endowments.

A third argument draws attention to the trajectory of relative economic growth when the income-growth line was going down (1970s and 1980s). Kerala was not an income-poor state that did the right things with health and education, as the proponents of the Kerala Model said. It was *becoming* poorer. The capitalism of the earlier era was weakening in the 1970s. Government policy made it weak through wrongheaded interventions in the business and agricultural sectors. Prior commitments made to schools and hospitals were maintained but were slowly leading the state to an inevitable fiscal crisis in the 1990s. States earn revenues by taxing market activity, and market activity was not in good shape.

In this backdrop of a gathering crisis, the second phase of the growth line becomes an interesting phenomenon. Why did a reversal happen from the early 1990s? Why did the factors that caused the falling behind become less forceful? We need to connect the two phases to explain the forging ahead in recent decades. Proponents of the enlightened state theory attribute the turnaround to human development. This is unpersuasive and an assertion. Why did we see a falling behind if there was a causal link between the two? Private investment, we argue, led the recent growth. Attrition of private investment caused the falling behind. Any account that omits to show how private investment fell and rose again is incomplete.

The explanation offered here concentrates on two processes unfolding since the late 1970s. One was mass migration for jobs and inward remittances, first to consumption and construction and later to investment, mainly in services. The second was the emergence of a technically skilled diaspora that invested in medium-scale industrial firms using some of the same resource advantages on which the princely-era capitalism was based. The new fields – spice extracts, Ayurvedic products, rubber products or packaged food – involved more scientific capital and capability than did the princely-era enterprises. In many cases, diasporic contacts with North America and Europe reinforced this capability. Global exposure has also been critical to the growth of information technology businesses since the 2000s.

As private investment revived, it generated other forms of business targeting local consumption. The high streets of most towns in the state have changed unrecognisably in the last thirty years. The shopping malls, mobile phone displays, automobile showrooms, swanky restaurants and bars do not directly reflect an external driver like Gulf money. It is endogenous to the resurgence of investment, high wages, an educated workforce that has considerable experience working abroad and, increasingly, low-wage semi-skilled migrant workers from eastern and northeastern states who populate the entire hospitality industry and specialised fields of labour such as jewellery, plywood and construction.

Several elements of the whole story – a state that overstretched itself with welfare spending, a left movement that scared and drove away private investors, and the revival of market activity after neoliberal reforms that strengthened job growth and public finances, if at the cost of inequality and environmental destruction – are common between Kerala and several other states of India. The effect was dramatic and concentrated in the state because of the enormous scale and many-sided legacies of the remittance economy.

What about Politics?

When we think generally about regimes in the state, the communists loom large. This is understandable, not only because of the long shelf life the movement has had in the state but also because the communists represented a certain manner of rule that left an impression on state capacity and state–market relationship.

The leftist regimes did many things right. They held the spending on health and education. The state's advance in healthcare was no doubt one of the foundations of a later stride in speciality healthcare, though in the sphere of education no such progression can be seen. The left ideology was deeply committed to the public distribution of food. A near-universal system of public distribution of food insulated the state from repeated agricultural shocks. The decentralised governance idea was pursued with resolve, and it will potentially deliver a better distribution of public welfare and create feedback between governance and service delivery. The left regimes also did some wrong things: destroying private capital, nearly destroying conventional agriculture, weakening growth and creating the conditions for a fiscal crisis.

During the recent turnaround, a symbiosis between private investment and leftist ideology took shape. The capitalist resurgence served public commitments. Capitalism helped communism in two ways. First, in the 2000s, the revival of market activity delivered more revenues. Second, from the 2000s, the state had more space to prioritise infrastructure development without reducing social sector expenditure, because private providers were also contributing to education and health. Private schools, technical schools, hospitals and medical service providers expanded so rapidly that the state became a major destination for health tourism worldwide. Without Gulf money, the Kerala Model would be long dead. To sustain the Kerala Model, the state needed to imaginatively integrate its economy with the world economy, neither through commodity transactions nor service and people transactions, but a combination of both.

The tax gains were modest and did not last long. Still, the two cushions vitally assisted the regime, which has been left-led since 2016. It could concentrate on welfare measures targeting inequality, decentralisation of governance, infrastructure spending and environmental protection. Inequality always figured prominently in the leftist agenda; indeed, it was almost fundamental to that agenda. This was the case in the 1930s when a communist movement formed in the region. That agenda has sustained the continued popularity of the left in the state, though the pattern of inequality targeted and forms of intervention changed.

The Future

The story helps us to offer some informed speculation on where the state is headed in the future. The state's capitalism stands, among others, on a unique strength. Most small Indian towns lack a good quality of life, measured in access to good healthcare, schools, roads, clean and plentiful common spaces, clean water, safety for women on the roads, retail trades and skilled services. In this state, the small towns are strikingly better off in these respects and not very different from the larger towns. In terms of cuisine and alcohol consumption in public, these places are less culturally inhibited than a town in Uttar Pradesh or West Bengal. The safety of women workers is, by and large, better than in north India. Its ability to draw in skilled and unskilled migrants is considerable. The state does not have many competitors in natural-resource-based sectors and investment in services such as tourism that exploit the combination of mountains and plentiful water. That is, the risk that investment dedicated to these fields would shift to another state is minimal. The forging ahead in economic growth is likely to continue for some more time.

On the other hand, there are huge, underutilised opportunities to use the state's unique advantages. The Kerala Model was good with primary education and an abject failure with higher education. The entry of private investment has not done much to improve the awful state of the universities and colleges. Private investment in education has revived, as in other states. However, private investors in education rarely understand how to build quality and target quantity instead. Bureaucrats are not competent to perform the complicated task of improving the quality of education. Most of them believe government officers know how to deliver quality education because the budget pays teachers' salaries. That is a mistake.

Long-time neglect of quality in higher education has essentially built a for-Kerala-by-Kerala type of higher education system, breeding mediocrity. This situation not only passes up a chance to sell quality education to potential students from outside the state, even abroad, but also disserves the skilling of the domestic workforce. The much-hyped syndrome of educated unemployment in the state owes largely to this failure. The growing knowledge economy sector in the state will continue to open opportunities for skilling and global integration for the domestic labour market. But how far the state can assure the participation of the relatively marginalised in this enterprise and make the process inclusive remains open to doubt.

The education quality challenge is largely overlooked in an otherwise active media. But the other big-time challenges are well known to scholars. One of them is environmental. Tourism and climate change threaten an environment with mountains, forests and water bodies dominating a larger part of the landmass than most Indian states. Excessive pressure on the common spaces is not happening in this one place alone. But the nature of the force is rather unique and, in some cases, more intense because the state tried to tout these assets to tourists. Elevated disaster risk does not owe to population growth or industrialisation but to constructing private dwellings and services like trade and tourism. Levels of living and a successful return to comparative advantage exposed the state to environmental and livelihood risks.

There are other challenges before the state. It has the most rapidly ageing society in India. India as such has a youngish population; the age of an average working Indian is 29. It is 37 in Kerala, of a similar order as China and the United States. The ageing population demands big adjustments in healthcare, social infrastructure and welfare provisions, including pensions. Further, in the matter of centre–state financial devolution, the reduced population growth creates an anomaly. With changes in the Finance Commission criteria concerning population, the five south Indian states assert that they are penalised for their better performance as they have reduced population growth. The state could lose a significant share of the devolution it had been receiving.

Government investment policy has found a compatibility with private enterprise that did not exist in the 1950s and 1960s. However, building urban infrastructure is expensive. So far, increasingly debt-funded, the funding trajectory is a knife edge. Massive investments have been made in modern infrastructure, including education, but to what extent they have been capable of addressing the increasing educated unemployment in the state or delivering skills remains open to question. Recently, the government's priorities have shifted towards environmental and infrastructural challenges. It is not so apparent whether it can muster the money to carry out action plans that take a long time to deliver benefits.

References

Abraham, Anu. 'International Migration, Return Migration and Occupational Mobility: Evidence from Kerala, India'. *Indian Journal of Labour Economics* 63, no. 5 (2020): 1223–43.

Abraham, Julie, Sibasis Hense and Elezebeth Mathews. 'Changing Social Dynamics and Older Population: A Qualitative Analysis of the Quality of Life among Older Adults in Kerala'. *Journal of Geriatric Mental Health* 9, no. 1 (2022): 34–42.

Achuthamenon, C. 'Keralathinoru Masterplan'. Pamphlet published by Prabhat Book House, Thiruvananthapuram, 1957.

Albin, Alice. 'Manufacturing Sector in Kerala: Comparative Study of Its Growth and Structure'. *Economic and Political Weekly* 25, no. 37 (1990): 2059–70.

Alexander, K. C. 'Emerging Farmer–Labour Relations in Kuttanad'. *Economic and Political Weekly* 8, no. 34 (1973): 1551–60.

Aneja, Ranjan and Anandu Praveen. 'International Migration Remittances and Economic Growth in Kerala: An Econometric Analysis'. *Journal of Public Affairs* 22, no. 1 (2022): 1–10.

Ansari, J. H. 'A Study of Settlement Patterns in Kerala'. *Ekistics* 30, no. 180 (1970): 427–35.

Arun, Shoba. '"We Are Farmers Too": Agrarian Change and Gendered Livelihoods in Kerala, South India'. *Journal of Gender Studies* 21, no. 3: (2012) 271–84.

———. 'Does Land Ownership Make a Difference? Women's Roles in Agriculture in Kerala, India'. *Gender and Development* 7, no. 3 (1999): 19–27.

Athukorala, Prema-Chandra. 'Review of K. C. Zachariah, K. P. Kannan and S. Irudaya Rajan, eds., *Kerala's Gulf Connection: CDS Studies on International Labour Migration from Kerala State in India*, Thiruvananthapuram: Centre for Development Studies, 2002'. *Journal of Asian Studies* 62, no. 4 (2003): 1311–13.

Azad, P., A. Abdul Salim and P. K. Sujathan. 'Has Emigration Perked Up Entrepreneurship Among Return Migrants in Kerala? Findings from a Survey in a High Migration Density District'. *Indian Journal of Labour Economics* 64, no. 5 (2021): 769–86.

Balakrishnan, Pulapre. 'Imagining an Economy of Plenty in Kerala'. *Economic and Political Weekly* 43, no. 20 (2008): 14–16.

Barbora, Sanjay, Susan Thieme, Karin Astrid Siegmann, Vineetha Menon and Ganesh Gurung. 'Migration Matters in South Asia: Commonalities and Critiques'. *Economic and Political Weekly* 43, no. 24 (2008): 57–65.

Bhagwati, Jagdish. 'Anti-globalization: Why?' *Journal of Policy Modeling* 26, no. 4 (2004): 439–63.

Bhalla, Ruchi and Surendra Meher. 'Education, Employment and Economic Growth with Special Reference to Females in Kerala'. *Indian Journal of Labour Economics* 62, no. 5 (2019): 639–65.

Brown, Hilton. *Parry's of Madras: A Story of British Enterprise in India.* Madras: Parry & Co., 1954.

Czaikay, Mathias and Maria Villares Varelaz. 'Labour Market Activity, Occupational Change and Length of Stay in the Gulf'. *Migration Studies* 3, no. 3 (2015): 315–42.

Damodaran, Sumangala. '"Women" Versus "Breadwinners": Exploring Labour Market Dynamics, Agency and Identity among Migrant Nurses from Kerala (India)'. *Global Labour Journal* 4, no. 3 (2013): 186–205.

Das Gupta. Ashin, *Malabar in Asian Trade, 1740–1800.* New York: Cambridge University Press, 1967.

Dasgupta, Dipankar, Pradip Maiti, Robin Mukherjee, Subrata Sarkar and Subhendu Chakrabarti. 'Growth and Interstate Disparities in India'. *Economic and Political Weekly* 35, no. 27 (2000), 2413–22.

Devassy, Seena. 'Wealth and Social Assertion: A Study on the Self-Assertion Movements of Syrian Christians, 1900–1950'. *Proceedings of the Indian History Congress* 75 (2014): 798–807.

Devika, J. 'Women's Labour, Patriarchy and Feminism in Twenty-first Century Kerala: Reflections on the Glocal Present'. *Review of Development and Change* 24, no. 1 (2019): 79–99.

Dhanagare, D. N. 'Agrarian Conflict, Religion and Politics: The Moplah Rebellions in Malabar in the Nineteenth and Early Twentieth Centuries'. *Past and Present* 74 (1977): 112–41.

Dhanesh, Ganga. 'Kerala. *God's Own Country*: From Backwaters to One of the Ten Paradises on Earth'. In *Public Relations Cases: International Perspectives,* edited by Danny Moss, Melanie Powerll and Barbara DeSanto, 40–58. Abingdon: Routledge, 2010.

Drèze, Jean and Amartya Sen. *An Uncertain Glory: India and Its Contradictions.* Princeton: Princeton University Press, 2013.

Dubey, Amaresh. 'Intra-State Disparities in Gujarat, Haryana, Kerala, Orissa and Punjab'. *Economic and Political Weekly,*44, nos. 26/27 (2009): 224–30.

Eapen, Mridul. 'Rural Non-Agricultural Employment in Kerala: Some Emerging Tendencies'. *Economic and Political Weekly* 29, no. 21 (1994): 1285–96.

Eswaran, K. K. 'Reemergence of Land Leasing in Kerala: The Case of Kuttanad'. *Social Scientist* 18, nos. 11/12 (1990): 64–80.

Franke, Richard and Barbara Chasin. 'Kerala: Development Without Growth'. *Earth Island Journal* 7, no. 2 (1992): 25–26.

George, Justin and Akhil Menon. 'The Withering of Kerala's Higher Education Sector? Concerns, Choices and the Way Forward'. *Indian Journal of Human Development*, Early view 17, no. 2 (2023): 380–85.

George, K. K. *Limits to Kerala Model of Development: An Analysis of Fiscal Crisis and Its Implications.* Trivandrum: Centre for Development Studies, 1993.

George, P. S. 'Emerging Trends in Size Distribution of Operational Holdings in Kerala'. *Economic and Political Weekly* 21, no. 5 (1986): 198–200.

George, Tijo, Mala Ramanathan and Udaya Shankar Mishra. 'Nature and Composition of InterState Migration into Districts of Kerala: Some Evidence from Census of India, 2011'. *Journal of Social and Economic Development* 24, no. 3 (2022): 379–403.

Gopinathan Nair, P. R. 'Decline in Birth Rate in Kerala: A Hypothesis about the Inter-Relationship between Demographic Variables, Health Services and Education'. *Economic and Political Weekly* 9, nos. 6–8 (1974): 323–36.

Government of India. *Census of India, 1951: Travancore-Cochin.* New Delhi: Government of India, 1953.

———. *Report of the Expert Group to Review the Methodology for Measurement of Poverty, Planning Commission.* New Delhi: Government Press, 2014.

———. *Statistical Abstracts for British India.* London: HMSO, 1901–04.

Government of Kerala. *Debt and Investment in Kerala.* Thiruvananthapuram: Department of Economics and Statistics, Government of Kerala, 2013.

———. *Kerala State Urbanisation Report.* Thiruvananthapuram: Local Self Government Department, 2012.

———. *Report of the Committee on Risk Transfer Mechanism for Disaster Risk Financing.* Government of Kerala, 2021.

————. *Report of the Task Force on Land Reforms and Agrarian Institutions.* Trivandrum: State Planning Board, 1997.

Government of Kerala and UNDP. *Post Disaster Needs Assessment: Floods and Landslides.* Thiruvananthapuram: Government of Kerala, 2019.

Gulati, Leela. 'Male Migration to Middle East and the Impact on the Family: Some Evidence from Kerala'. *Economic and Political Weekly* 18, nos. 52–53 (1983): 2217–26.

————. 'Migration and Social Change in Kerala'. *India International Centre Quarterly* 22, nos. 2/3 (1995): 191–202.

Harilal, K. N. and K. J. Joseph. 'Stagnation and Revival of Kerala Economy: An Open Economy Perspective'. Working Paper of Centre for development Studies (Trivandrum), 2000.

Herring, Ronald J. *Land to the Tiller: The Political Economy of Agrarian Reform in South Asia.* Delhi, Oxford University Press, 1983.

Herring, Ronald. 'Embedded Particularism: India's Failed Developmental State'. In *The Developmental State*, edited by Meredith Woo-Cumings, 306–34. Ithaca, NY: Cornell University Press, 1999.

Hill, Polly. 'Kerala Is Different'. *Modern Asian Studies* 20, no. 4 (1986): 779–92.

Ibrahim, P. 'The Development of Transport Facilities in Kerala: A Historical Review'. *Social Scientist* 6, no. 8 (1978): 34–48.

Imran Khan, M. and C. Valatheeswaran. 'International Migration, Remittances and Labour Force Participation of Left-behind Family Members: A Study of Kerala'. *Margin—The Journal of Applied Economic Research* 10, no. 1 (2016): 86–118.

Irudaya Rajan, S. 'From Kerala to the Gulf: Impacts of Labor Migration'. *Asian and Pacific Migration Journal* 13, no. 4 (2004): 497–509.

Irudaya Rajan, S., Aneeta Shajan and S. Sunitha. 'Ageing and Elderly Care in Kerala'. *China Report* 56, no. 3 (2020): 354–73.

Jeffrey, Robin. 'Temple-Entry Movement in Travancore, 1860–1940'. *Social Scientist* 4, no. 8 (1976): 3–27.

————. *The Decline of Nayar Dominance: Society and Politics in Travancore, 1847–1908.* New Delhi: Vikas, 1976.

————. *Politics, Women and Well-Being. How Kerala Became a Model.* Basingstoke: Palgrave Macmillan, 1992.

Jeromi, P. D., 'Economic Reforms in Kerala'. *Economic and Political Weekly* 40, no. 30 (2005): 3267–77.

———. 'Farmers' Indebtedness and Suicides: Impact of Agricultural Trade Liberalisation in Kerala'. *Economic and Political Weekly* 42, no. 31 (2007): 3241–47.

———. 'What Ails Kerala's Economy: A Sectoral Exploration'. *Economic and Political Weekly* 38, no. 16 (2003): 1584–1600.

Jose, M. and M. Padmanabhan. 'Dynamics of Agricultural Land Use Change in Kerala: A Policy and Social-ecological Perspective'. *International Journal of Agricultural Sustainability* 14, no. 3 (2016): 307–24.

Joseph, Brigit and K. J. Joseph. 'Commercial Agriculture in Kerala after the WTO'. *South Asia Economic Journal* 6, no. 37 (2005): 37–57.

Joseph, John. 'Peasant Migration to Malabar with a Special Reference to Peravoor Settlment (1925–1970)'. *Proceedings of the Indian History Congress* 69 (2008): 1178–87.

Joseph, Sebastian. 'Slave Labour of Malabar in the Colonial Context'. *Proceedings of the Indian History Congress* 45 (1984): 694–703.

Kannan, K. P. 'Agricultural Development in an Emerging Non-Agrarian Regional Economy: Kerala's Challenges'. *Economic and Political Weekly* 46, no. 9 (2011): 64–70.

———. 'Employment, Wages, and Conditions of Work in the Cashew Processing Industry'. Working Paper of Centre for Development Studies (Trivandrum), 1978.

———. 'Kerala Economy at the Crossroads?' *Economic and Political Weekly* 25, nos. 35–36 (1990): 1951–56.

———. 'Kerala "Model" of Development Revisited: A Sixty-Year Assessment of Successes and Failures'. *Indian Economic Journal* 71, no. 1 (2023): 120–51.

———. 'Kerala's Turnaround in Growth: Role of Social Development, Remittances and Reform'. *Economic and Political Weekly* 40, no. 6 (2005): 548–54.

Kannan, K. P. and K. S. Hari. 'Revisiting Kerala's Gulf Connection: Half a Century of Emigration, Remittances and Their Macroeconomic Impact, 1972–2020'. *Indian Journal of Labour Economics* 63, no. 4 (2020): 941–67.

K. P. Kannan and P. Pushpangadan. 'Dissecting Agricultural Stagnation in Kerala: An Analysis across Crops, Seasons and Regions'. *Economic and Political Weekly* 25, nos. 35–36 (1990): 1991–2004.

Karinkurayil, Mohamed Shafeeq. 'The Days of Plenty: Images of First Generation Malayali Migrants in the Arabian Gulf'. *South Asian Diaspora*. 13, no. 1 (2021): 51–64.

Kerala State Council for Science, Technology and Environment (KSCSTE). *Committee to Examine the Causes of Repeated Extreme Heavy Rainfall Events, Subsequent Floods and Landslides and to Recommend Appropriate Policy Responses*. Thiruvananthapuram: Government of Kerala, 2019.

———.*State of the Environment Report – Kerala 2007: Volume 2, Natural Hazards*. Thiruvananthapuram: Government of Kerala, 2007.

Kerala State Planning Board. *Kerala Human Development Report* (2021). Thiruvananthapuram: Government of Kerala, 2021.

Kooiman, Dick. 'The Gospel of Coffee: Mission, Education and Employment in 19th Century Travancore'. *Economic and Political Weekly* 19, no. 35 (1984): 1535–44.

Kooria, Mahmood. 'Politics, Economy and Islam in "Dutch Ponnāni," Malabar Coast'. *Journal of the Economic and Social History of the Orient* 62, no. 1 (2019): 1–34.

Koshi, M. J. *K.C. Mammen Mappillai*. Trivandrum: Kerala Historical Society, 1976.

Krishna Kumar, S. and S. Irudaya Rajan. *Emigration in 21st-Century India: Governance, Legislation, Institutions*. New Delhi: Routledge, 2014.

Krishnan, T. N., 'Wages, Employment and Output in Interrelated Labour Markets in an Agrarian Economy: A Study of Kerala'. *Economic and Political Weekly* 26, no. 26 (1991): A82–A96.

Kuriakose, S. L., G. Sankar and C. Muraleedharan. 'History of Landslide Susceptibility and a Chorology of Landslide-Prone Areas in the Western Ghats of Kerala, India'. *Environmental Geology* 57, no. 7 (2019): 1553–68.

Kurien, C. T. 'Kerala's Development Experience: Random Comments about the past and Some Considerations for the Future'. *Social Scientist* 23, nos. 1–3 (1995): 50–69.

Langley, W. K. M. *A Century in Malabar: The History of Peirce Leslie and Co. Ltd. 1862–1962*. Madras: Associate Printers, 1962.

Lankina, Tila V. and Lullit Getachew. 'Competitive Religious Entrepreneurs: Christian Missionaries and Female Education in Colonial and Post-Colonial India'. *British Journal of Political Science* 43, no. 1 (2013): 103–31.

Lewandowski, Susan. *Migration and Ethnicity in Urban India: Kerala Migrants in the City of Madras, 1870–1970*. New Delhi: Manohar, 1980.

Lindberg, Anna. 'Child Marriage in Late Travancore: Religion, Modernity and Change'. *Economic and Political Weekly* 49, no. 17 (2014): 79–87.

Mahadevan, Raman. 'Industrial Entrepreneurship in Princely Travancore: 1930–47'. In *The South Indian Economy, Agrarian Change, Industrial*

Structure, and State Policy c. 1914–1947, edited by Sabyasachi Bhattacharya, Sumit Guha, Raman Mahadevan, Sakthi Padhi, D. Rajasekhar and G. N. Rao, 159–207. Delhi: Oxford University Press, 1991.

Mani, Sunil. 'Economic Liberalisation and Kerala's Industrial Sector: An Assessment of Investment Opportunities'. *Economic and Political Weekly* 31, no. 34 (1996): 2323–30.

Mani, Sunil and M. Arun. 'Liberalisation of Technical Education in Kerala: Has a Significant Increase in Enrolment Translated into Increase in Supply of Engineers?' Working Paper of Centre for Development Studies (Trivandrum), 2012.

Mann, Michael. 'Timber Trade on the Malabar Coast, c. 1780–1840'. *Environment and History* 7, no. 4 (2001): 403–25.

Mari Bhat, P. N. and S. Irudaya Rajan. 'Demographic Transition in Kerala Revisited'. *Economic and Political Weekly* 25, nos. 35–36 (1990): 1957–80.

Maruthur, Sumeetha Mokkil. 'Skill in a Globalized World: Migrant Workers in the Gold Jewelry-Making Industry in Kerala, India'. *Journal of Labor and Society* 17, no. 3 (2014): 323–38.

Mathew, Joshy. 'Plantation Economy in Colonial Malabar – With Special Reference to Wayanad'. *Proceedings of the Indian History Congress* 67 (2006–07): 730–37.

Mathew, P. M. 'Exploitation of Women Labour: An Analysis of Women's Employment in Kerala'. *Social Scientist* 13, nos. 10–11 (1985): 28–47.

Mencher, Joan P. 'Why Grow More Food? An Analysis of Some Contradictions in the "Green Revolution" in Kerala'. *Economic and Political Weekly* 13, nos. 51/52 (1978): A98–A104.

Menon, Dilip M. *Caste, Nationalism and Communism in South India. Malabar, 1900–1948.* Cambridge: Cambridge University Press, 1994.

Michael Tharakan, P. K. 'Dimensions and Characteristics of the Migration of Farmers from Travancore to Malabar, 1930–50'. *Journal of Kerala Studies* 5, no. 2 (1978): 287–89.

———. 'Socio-Economic Factors in Educational Development: Case of Nineteenth Century Travancore'. *Economic and Political Weekly* 19, no. 45 (1984): 1913–28.

Mohanan Pillai, P. 'Whither State Sector Enterprises in Kerala?' *Economic and Political Weekly* 25, nos. 7/8 (1990): M9–M16.

Nagam Aiya, V. *Travancore State Manual,* 2 vols. Trivandrum: Travancore Government Press, 1906.

Nair, Sreelekha. 'Rethinking Citizenship, Community and Rights: The Case of Nurses from Kerala in Delhi'. *Indian Journal of Gender Studies* 14, no. 1 (2007): 137–56.

Namboodiripad, E. M. S. *The Communist Party in Kerala: Six Decades of Struggle and Advance*. New Delhi: National Book Centre, 1994.

Narayana, D. and C. S. Venkiteswaran. 'Domestic Migrant Labour in Kerala'. Gulati Institute of Finance and Taxation, Thiruvananthapuram, 2013.

Neethi, P. 'Globalization Lived Locally: Investigating Kerala's Local Labour Control Regimes'. *Development and Change* 43, no. 6 (2012): 1239–63.

Nesamony, Sam. 'Missionaries, Literacy and Intellectual Consciousness in South Travancore'. *Proceedings of the Indian History Congress* 77 (2016): 651–64.

Oommen, Ginu Zacharia. 'South Asia–Gulf Migratory Corridor: Emerging Patterns, Prospects and Challenges'. *Migration and Development* 5, no. 3 (2015): —394–412.

Oommen, M. A. 'Mobility of Small Scale Entrepreneurs: A Kerala Experience'. *Indian Journal of Industrial Relations* 17, no. 1 (1981): 65–87.

———. 'Rise and Growth of Banking in Kerala'. *Social Scientist* 5, no. 3 (1976): 24–46.

Oommen, M. A., Sally Wallace and Abdu Muwonge. 'Towards Streamlining Panchayat Finance in India: A Study Based on Gram Panchayats in Kerala'. *Economic and Political Weekly* 52, no. 38 (2017): 49–58.

Osella, Caroline and Filippo Osella. 'Once upon a Time in the West? Stories of Migration and Modernity from Kerala, South India'. *Journal of the Royal Anthropological Institute* 12, no. 3 (2006): 569–88.

Padmanabhan, Nirmala. 'Poor Performance of Private Corporate Sector in Kerala'. *Economic and Political Weekly* 25, no. 37 (1990): 2071–75.

Panikar, P. G. K. 'Fall in Mortality Rates in Kerala: An Explanatory Hypothesis'. *Economic and Political Weekly* 10, no. 47 (1975): 1811–18.

———. 'Fertility Decline in Kerala: Social Justice Hypothesis'. *Economic and Political Weekly* 19, no. 13 (1984): 571–72.

Panikar, P. G. K. and C. R. Soman. *Health Status of Kerala: Paradox of Economic Backwardness and Health Development*. Trivandrum: Centre for Development Studies, 1984.

Parida, J. K, S. K. Mohanty and K. Ravi Raman. 'Remittances, Household Expenditure and Investment in Rural India: Evidence from NSS Data'. *Indian Economic Review* 50, no. 1 (2015): 79–104.

Parida, Jajati K. and K. Ravi Raman. *A Study on In-migration, Informal Employment and Urbanization in Kerala*. Thiruvanathapuram: Kerala State Planning Board, 2020.

Parida, Jajati K. and K. Ravi Raman. 'India: International and Internal Migration'. In *Migration and Globalization: Handbook*, edited by Anna Triandafyllidou, 226–46. Cheltenham: Edward Elgar, 2018.

Parida, Jajati K., Merry Elizabeth John and Justin Sunny. 'Construction Labour Migrants and Wage Inequality in Kerala'. *Journal of Social and Economic Development* 22, no. 4 (2020): 414–44.

Patnaik, Prabhat. 'The International Context and the "Kerala Model"'. *Social Scientist* 23, nos. 1/3 (1995): 37–49.

Pattadath, Bindhulakshmi. 'The Blurred Boundaries of Migration: Transnational Flows of Women Domestic Workers from Kerala to UAE'. *Social Change* 50, no. 1 (2020): 95–108.

Peter, Binoy. 'Labour Migration to Kerala: The Case of Plywood Industry'. PhD dissertation of International Institute for Population Sciences, Mumbai, 2010.

Pillai, V. R. and P. G. K. Panikar. *Land Reclamation in Kerala*. Bombay: Asia Publishing, 1965.

Prakash, B. A. 'Agrarian Kerala, Down the Centuries'. *State and Society* 5, no. 1 (1984): 61–84.

Prasad, G. and M. V. Ramesh. 'Spatio-temporal Analysis of Land Use/Land Cover Changes in an Ecologically Fragile Area—Alappuzha District, Southern Kerala, India'. *Natural Resources Research* 28, Supplement 1 (2019): 31–42.

Purayil, Mufsin Puthan and Manish Thakur. 'The Strength of Strong Ties: Wasta and Migration Strategies among the Mappila Muslims of Northern Kerala, India'. *Journal of Ethnic and Migration Studies* 49, no. 19 (2023): 5099–116.

Qadeer, Imrana. 'Giving Public Health Services More Than Their Due'. *Economic and Political Weekly* 22, no. 29 (1987): 1187–88.

Radhakrishnan, P. *Peasant Struggles, Land Reforms and Social Change: Malabar 1836–1982*. New Delhi: Sage, 1989.

Ram Mohan, K. T. 'Material Processes and Developmentalism: Interpreting Economic Change in Colonial Tiruvitamkur, 1800–1945'. PhD dissertation submitted to the Centre for Development Studies, 1996.

Rammohan, K. T., 'Assessing Reassessment of Kerala Model'. *Economic and Political Weekly* 35, no. 15 (2000): 1234–36.

———. 'Understanding Kerala: The Tragedy of Radical Scholarship'. *Monthly Review* 43, no. 7 (1991): 18–36.

Rammohan, K. T. and K. Ravi Raman. 'Of Cochin Stock Exchange and What It Means?' *Economic and Political Weekly* 25, no. 1 (1990): 17–19.

Ravi Raman, K. 'Asian Development Bank, Policy Conditionalities and the Social Democratic Governance: Kerala Model under Pressure?' *Review of International Political Economy* 16, no. 2 (2009): 284–308.

———. 'Breaking New Ground: Adivasi Land Struggle in Kerala'. *Economic and Political Weekly* 37, no. 10 (2002): 916–18.

———. 'Business, Ethnicity, Politics and Imperial Interests, UPASI'. *Business History Review* 88, no. 1 (2014): 73–95.

———. 'Corporate Violence, Legal Nuances and Political Ecology: Cola War in Plachimada'. *Economic and Political Weekly* 40, no. 25 (2005): 2481–86.

———. 'Currents and Eddies: Indian Middle East Migration Processes'. *Cambridge Journal of Regions, Economy and Society* 5, no. 2 (2011): 189–205.

——— (ed.). *Development, Democracy and the State: Critiquing Kerala Model of Development*. London and New York: Routledge, 2010.

———. 'Ecospatiality: Transforming Kerala's Post-flood Riskscapes'. *Cambridge Journal of Regions, Economy and Society* 13, no. 2 (2020): 319–41.

———. *Global Capital and Peripheral Labour: The History and Political Economy of Plantation Workers in India*. Abingdon: Routledge, 2010.

———. 'In-Migration vs Out-Migration'. In *Mass Migration in the World-System: Past, Present and Future*, edited by Terry-Ann Jones and Eric Mielants, 122–43. Abingdon: Routledge, 2011.

———. *Political Ecospatiality: Protests and Politics in Kerala*. Cambridge: Cambridge University Press, forthcoming.

———. 'Right-making Is State-making; State-making Is Right-making'. Labour Department Policy Series Publications, Government of Kerala, Thiruvananthapuram, 2023, 34–41.

———. 'Subaltern Modernity: Kerala, The Eastern Theatre of Resistance in The Global South'. *Sociology: British Association of Sociology* 51, no. 1 (2017): 91–110.

———. 'The Opposition "Emocracy" Exposed: Kerala's Landmark Left Victory'. *Monthly Review*, 15 October (2021). Available at https://mronline.org/2021/10/15/the-opposition-emocracy-exposed-keralas-landmark-left-victory/ (accessed 4 February 2024).

———. 'Transverse Solidarity: Water, Power and Resistance'. *Review of Radical Political Economics* 42, no. 2 (2010): 251–68.

Reddy, Sujani K. *Nursing and Empire: Gendered Labor and Migration from India to the United States*. Chapel Hill: University of North Carolina Press, 2015.

Roy, Tirthankar. *The Economy of South Asia*. London: Palgrave, 2016.

———. *An Economic History of India, 1707–1857*. Abingdon: Routledge, 2021.

Sajitha, A. 'Regional Variations in the Performance of Black Pepper Cultivation in Kerala: An Exploration of Non Price Factors'. Paper for National Research Programme on Plantation Development, Centre for Development Studies, Trivandrum, 2014.

Singh, Anjana. *Fort Cochin in Kerala, 1750–1830: The Social Condition of a Dutch Community in an Indian Milieu*. Leiden and Boston: Brill, 2010.

Sreekumar, T. T. and Govindan Parayil. 'Contentions and Contradictions of Tourism as Development Option: The Case of Kerala, India'. *Third World Quarterly* 23, no. 3 (2002): 529–48.

Sreelekha, R. G. 'Democracy and Development at the Grassroots People's Planning in Vithura Panchayat: A Case Study'. PhD dissertation, University of Kerala, 2014.

Sreeraj, A. P. and Vamsi Vakulabharanam. 'High Growth and Rising Inequality in Kerala since the 1980s'. *Oxford Development Studies* 44, no. 4 (2016): 367–83.

Sreerupa. 'Transnational Migration, Local Specificities and Reconfiguring Eldercare through "Market Transfer" in Kerala, India'. *Journal of Ethnic and Migration Studies* 49, no. 4 (2023): 1014–31.

Subrahmanian, K. K. and P. Mohanan Pillai. 'Kerala's Industrial Backwardness: Exploration of Alternative Hypotheses'. *Economic and Political Weekly* 21, no. 14 (1986): 577–92.

Sudheer, K. P., M. Bhallamudi, B. Narasimhan, J. Thomas, V. M. Bindhu, V. K. Vema and C. Kurian. 'Role of Dams on the Floods of August 2018 in Periyar River Basin, Kerala'. *Current Science* 116, no. 5 (2019): 780–94.

Sukumaran Nair, M. K. 'Rural Labour Market in Kerala: Small Holder Agriculture and Labour Market Dynamics'. *Economic and Political Weekly* 32, no. 35 (1997): L45–L52.

Thampy, M. M. 'Wage-Cost and Kerala's Industrial Stagnation: Study of Organised Small-Scale Sector'. *Economic and Political Weekly* 25, no. 37 (1990): 2077–82.

Tharian George, K. 'The Crisis of the South Indian Tea Industry: Legacy of the Control by British Tea Multinationals'. Working Paper of Centre for Development Studies (Trivandrum), 1984.

Tharian George, K., V. Haridasan and B. Sreekumar. 'Role of Government and Structural Changes in Rubber Plantation Industry'. *Economic and Political Weekly* 23, no. 48 (1988): M158–M166.

Thomas Isaac, T. M. 'Class Struggle and Structural Changes: Coir Mat and Matting Industry in Kerala, 1950–80'. *Economic and Political Weekly* 17, no. 31 (1982): PE13–PE29.

Thomas Isaac, T. M. and P. K. Michael Tharakan. 'An Inquiry into the Historical Roots of Industrial Backwardness of Kerala: A Study of Travancore Region'. Working Paper of Centre for Development Studies (Trivandrum), 1986.

Thomas, Jayan Jose. 'Kerala's Industrial Backwardness: A Case of Path Dependence in Industrialization?' *World Development* 33, no. 5 (2005): 763–83.

———. 'The Achievements and Challenges of the Kerala "Model"'. *India Forum*. Available at https://www.theindiaforum.in/article/achievements-challenges-kerala-model (accessed 1 February 2024).

Thomas, K. T., 'The Commercialisation of Agriculture and 19th Century Agrarian Relations in Malabar'. *Proceedings of the Indian History Congress* 58 (1997): 668–76.

———. 'The Hidden Agenda in a Welfare Garb: Socio-Economic Reforms in Travancore (19th C.)'. *Proceedings of the Indian History Congress* 66 (2005–06): 949–57.

Thomas, Neethu and D. Shyjan. 'Outsiders of the Labour Force in Kerala: Demystifying Deterrents of Female Work'. *Indian Journal of Labour Economics* 65, no. 2 (2022): 445–61.

Thomas, Susan. 'Judicial Interventions and Changes in the Malabar "Nayar Taravads" during the Colonial Period'. *Proceedings of the Indian History Congress, 2000–2001* 61, Part I (2000–01): 945–53.

Timmons, Stephen, Catrin Evans and Sreelekha Nair. 'The Development of the Nursing Profession in a Globalised Context: A Qualitative Case Study in Kerala, India'. *Social Science and Medicine* 166 (2016): 41–48.

United Nations. *Poverty, Unemployment and Development Policy: A Case Study of Selected Issues with Reference to Kerala*. New York: United Nations, 1975.

Varma, Divya and Benoy Peter. 'Labour Migration to Kerala: Challenges, Opportunities and Need for an Institutional Response'. Available at https://www.shram.org/uploadFiles/20170627122555.pdf (accessed 2 February 2024).

Velu Pillai, T. K. *The Travancore State Manual* (4 vols.), vol. 3. Trivandrum: Government Press, 1940.

Wood, Conrad. 'The Moplah Rebellion of 1921–22 and Its Genesis'. PhD dissertation of School of Oriental and African Studies, London, 1975.

Zachariah, K. C. and S. Irudaya Rajan. 'Inflexion in Kerala's Gulf Connection: Report on Kerala Migration Survey 2011'. Working Paper of the Centre for Development Studies, Thiruvananthapuram, 2012.

Zachariah, K. C., P. R. Gopinathan Nair and S. Irudaya Rajan. 'Return Emigrants in Kerala: Rehabilitation Problems and Development Potential'. Working paper, Centre for Development Studies, Thiruvananthapuram, 2001.

Index

Abad Fisheries, 70
Abdul Salim, A., 90
Abraham, Anu, 89
Abraham, Julie, 109
Achuthamenon, C., 119, 121, 123, 125
Active Char, 72
Adivasi, 122, 124–126, 140
Agappe, 75, 77–78
agriculture, 11, 13, 20–23, 25, 28–29,
    39–55, 57, 65, 72, 83, 91, 108–12,
    120, 130, 137–38, 140, 147
Ajmal, V. A., 77
Akay Natural Ingredients, 71
Alappuzha (Alleppey), 28, 45, 56, 76,
    138–39
Albin, Alice, 60
Alexander, K. C., 44
Alleppey, 28, 45, 56, 76, 138–39
Alukkas, Varghese, 79
Aluva (Alwaye), 56
Andhra Pradesh, 7, 129
Aneja, Ranjan, 87
Anglo-Mysore wars, 18–20
Ansari, J. H., 42
Arabia, 17, 84
Arabian Sea, 10–11, 134
areca nut, 23–24, 73
Arjuna Natural Extracts, 71–72
Arun, Shoba, 54, 91

Arya Vaidya Sala, 69
Aspinwall, 23, 28
Athukorala, Prema-Chandra, 86, 96
AVT, 72
ayurveda, 68–69
Ayyankali, 35
Azad, P., 90

Balakrishnan, Pulapre, 124
Bangladesh, 84
banking, 4, 25, 27–30, 44, 51, 56–57,
    62, 63, 86, 88, 93–94, 112, 126
Barbora, Sanjay, 85
Beypur, 17, 26
Bhagwati, Jagdish, 99
Bhallamudi, M., 142
Bhalla, Ruchi, 94
Bhattacharya, S., 30
Bindhu, V. M., 142
birth rate, 104–07, 109. *See also* fertility
Bismi, 77
BKPL, 137
Bombay, 24, 36, 44, 83, 137
Brahmins, 32, 37
Bramma, 77
British, 2, 6, 10, 16–22, 24–26, 28,
    30–33, 35–36, 38–40, 58, 65,
    83, 100–02, 104–05, 123, 130, 135,
    140

British India, 6, 16, 19, 20, 22, 25–26, 32, 35–36, 38–40, 83, 100–02, 104–05

Burma, 70, 129–30

business, 23–30

Calicut (Kozhikkode), 17–19, 24, 79, 120, 128, 137–38, 140–41

capitalism, 14, 40, 66–67, 77–81, 95–96, 118, 132, 138, 145–47

cardamom, 23, 64–65, 71, 80, 139

Cardamom Hill Reserve Area, 139

Careon, 75

Carnatic state, 18

cashew, 10, 23–24, 27, 46, 53, 56, 58, 60–61, 63, 65, 70–71, 74, 76, 80

caste, 4, 11, 13, 20–22, 25, 31–34, 38–40, 42–44, 51–52, 63, 94–95, 97, 106, 115–17, 119, 122, 125, 127, 132. *See also* Nayars, Nambudris, Dalits, Scheduled Caste

Centre for Development Studies, 4, 12, 26, 28, 30, 58, 62, 64, 76, 87, 89–90, 105, 109

Chakrabarti, Subhendu, 8

Chasin, Barbara, 3

child marriages, 37

Christian, 6, 24, 26–27, 29, 31–34, 37–40, 43–44, 63–64, 70, 102, 115, 117, 119, 127

church, 6, 24, 33–34, 38, 56, 89, 101–02, 127

climate, 2, 10, 28–29, 53, 114, 134–35, 148

Clinical Establishment Bill, 129

Cochin (Kochi), 16–20, 22–23, 28–29, 36, 56, 62–63, 68, 70–71, 73–75, 81, 104, 121, 128, 130, 136, 140, 144–45

Cochin state, 16, 18, 22–23, 29

coconut, 10, 23–25, 39–40, 44–45, 52–53, 58, 64, 70, 72, 74, 78, 139

coir, 10, 25, 27–28, 31, 46, 56, 58–61, 63, 65, 72, 80, 136

communism, 33, 132, 147

communist parties, 13, 33, 45–46, 118–19, 121, 132

comparative advantage, 2, 14, 53, 62–63, 80–81, 149

construction, 14, 23, 43, 49–50, 62, 66, 73, 76–77, 79, 82, 84, 90, 95, 97, 112, 125, 135–36, 143, 145–46

Covid-19, 55, 131

CPI, 119–22

CPI(M), 119

Czaikay, Mathias, 98

Dalits, 13, 51, 124, 126, 140

Damodaran, Sumangala, 93

Darragh Smail and Co., 28

Dasgupta, Dipankar, 8

death rates, 104–06, 108

debt to asset ratio (DAR), 116

decentralisation, 13, 103, 120, 130–32, 147

deforestation, 135–37, 139–40, 142

democracy and decentralisation, 130–32

demographic transition, 6, 11, 83, 104–09, 133

DentCare, 75

Devika, J., 92

Dhanagare, D. M., 16–17

Dominic, Jose, 69

Dréze, Jean, 7, 99

droughts, 6, 10, 14, 28–29, 55, 103, 105–06, 134

Dubey, Amaresh, 8

Dutch business, 19–20

Dutch disease, 62

Eapen, Mridul, 50, 66
East India Company, 10, 19
education, 3, 6–7, 12–14, 31–35, 37–38,
    40, 76, 78–79, 82–83, 87–88, 90,
    92–95, 99–103, 106–10, 112–14, 117,
    120–21, 127–28, 132–33, 144–49.
    See also higher education
Education Bill, 121, 127
environment, 14, 24, 55, 103, 105–06,
    114, 118, 133–37, 139, 141–43,
    145–49
epidemic, 6, 103, 105
Ernakulam, 56, 69, 73, 96, 128
Eswaran, K. K., 48
Europe, 10, 12, 24, 27, 146
European capital, 26
Evans, Catrin, 94

famines, 6, 10, 105–06
fertility, 11, 92, 100, 104, 106–08, 117
Fertilizer and Chemical Travancore
    Limited (FACT), 136
film industry, 66
finance, 4, 11, 27, 29, 30, 36, 51–52, 54,
    56, 65, 74, 77, 92, 97, 99, 112–14,
    118, 132, 146, 149
Finlay, James, 27–28, 64
First Left Government, 120–22
fishing, 51, 97
floods, 14, 27, 42, 44, 55, 74, 131, 135,
    141–43
foreign investment, 10, 12, 20, 23, 25,
    59, 62, 67, 69, 72, 77, 79, 81
Francis, K. L., 70
Franke, Richard, 3, 7
French, 18, 19, 68

Galfar, 72
GDP, 3, 7, 10
George, Justine, 102
George, K. K., 4

George, Tijo, 96
Getachew, Lullit, 38, 102
ginger, 23, 41
globalization, 4, 10–11, 34, 80–82, 94,
    98, 102
gold, 67, 73–74, 77–79, 97–98
Gold Control Order, 74
Gopalakrishnan, Senapathy, 76
Gopinathan Nair, P. R., 89, 107
Green Revolution, 42, 46–47
gross domestic product, 3, 7, 10.
    See also GDP
Gujarat, 1, 8, 80–81, 144
Gulati, Leela, 91–92, 97
Gulf, 8–9, 11–12, 43, 47, 49–50, 62,
    66–67, 69, 73–75, 77–79, 81–93,
    95–96, 98, 130, 134–35, 146–47
Guru, Narayana, 35
Gurung, Ganesh, 85

handloom weaving, 27, 63
Hari, K. S., 90
Harrisons Malayalam, 123
Harrisons and Crosfield, 28
Hashim, Usman Mohammed, 70
healthcare, 3, 11, 14, 75, 79–80, 89,
    93, 100, 103–04, 112–13, 117, 125,
    128–29, 133, 144–47, 149
Hense, Sibasis, 109
Herring, Ronald, 123–24
higher education, 12, 32, 35, 82–83,
    94–95, 102, 114, 148
Hill, Polly, 1–2
Hindalco, 137
Hindu, 13, 21–22, 31, 37, 39, 43–44,
    115, 117, 136–37
Hyder Ali, 17–18, 20
hydroelectric power, 29–30, 114, 135

Imran Khan, M., 88
India Migration Reports, 82

Indian Rare Earth (IRE) Limited, 136
industrialisation, 29–30, 56–57, 61–62, 65, 80, 135, 137–38, 149
industrial pollution, 135–37
inequality, 2–3, 6, 8–9, 12–14, 16, 21, 30–33, 44, 57, 97, 100, 102–03, 114–18, 122, 124, 127, 130, 132–33, 144, 146–47
information technology, 12, 67, 69, 113, 146
Infosys, 76
Integrated Child Development Scheme (ICDS), 104, 130
Irudaya Rajan, S., 6, 86–90, 92–93, 109

Jacob, C. V., 71, 73
Jeffrey, Robin, 31–32, 39
Jeromi, P. D., 4, 9, 52
Jews, 17
John, Baby, 123
John, Merry Elizabeth, 97
John, Thomas, 75
Jose, M., 138
Joseph, Sebastian, 31
Joy Alukkas, 79
Jyothy Labs, 75

Kalyan Jewellers, 74, 77
Kanam Latex, 75
Kannan Devan, 64, 72, 123, 125
Kannan, K. P., 9, 47, 54, 58, 64–65, 72, 86, 90, 123, 125
Karinkurayil, Mohamed Shafeeq, 98
Karnataka, 1, 7, 109
Karunakaran, K., 131
Kerala Association for Nonformal Education and Development, 128
Kerala Land Utilization Act, 45–46
Kerala Migration Survey, 12, 82, 90

Kerala Model, 4, 5, 7–9, 60, 77–78, 80, 86–87, 95, 100, 106, 117, 131, 133, 145, 147–48
Kerala Shastra Sahitya Parishad (KSSP), 128, 131–32
Kerala State Council for Science Technology and Environment (KSCSTE), 103, 142
Kerala State Disaster Management Plan, 142
Kerala Stay of Eviction Proceedings Act, 121
Kitex Garments, 73
Kochi, 18, 68, 70–71, 73–75, 81, 140. See also Cochin
Kollam (Quilon), 29, 56, 70, 76, 79–80, 136
Kooiman, Dick, 34
Korah, Geemon, 71
Kozhikode (Calicut), 17–19, 24, 79, 120, 128, 137–38, 140–41
Krishna Kumar, S., 88, 93
Kudumbashree, 131
Kunjachan, P. J., 72
Kuriakose, John, 75
Kurian, C., 142
Kurian, Varghese, 79
Kurien, C. T., 57, 61
Kuttanad, 44, 46, 48–49, 55, 139

labour, 6, 11–13, 15, 21, 25–26, 28, 30–34, 40–51, 53, 57–58, 62–64, 73, 76–77, 79–98, 100, 102, 108, 114–15, 119, 124, 126–27, 133, 136–38, 143, 146, 148
landed property, 20–23
land reclamation, 43–44
land reform, 42–43, 45–47, 49, 64, 108, 111, 119, 121–26, 132
land use, 135–42
Lankina, Tomila, 38, 102

left movement, 13, 33, 118, 132, 146.
    See also communism, communist
    parties, CPI, CPI(M)
left politics, 13, 42, 45, 132

life expectancy, 5–7, 103, 106, 114, 134,
    144
Lindberg, Anna, 37
literacy rate, 2–3, 101, 114, 128
Lukose, Mary Punnen, 128
Lulu, 75

Madhava Rao, T., 20
Madras, 19, 28, 33, 36, 83
Madras Presidency, 16, 38, 129
Mahadevan, Raman, 30
Maharashtra, 56, 72
Mahé, 18
Maiti, Pradip, 8
Malabar, 6, 10, 16–28, 30–33, 37, 40,
    43, 63, 69–70, 73, 84, 104, 121–22,
    127–30, 135
Malankara Plantations, 64
Malayalam Plantation, 123
Mammen Mappillai, K. C., 29
Mane Kancor, 71
Mani, Sunil, 57, 61, 66, 76
Mann, Michael, 24
Mappila, 20–21, 84–85
Mari Bhat, P. N., 6
Maruthur, Sumeetha Mokkil, 98
Mathew, Joshy, 27
Mathew, P. M., 57
Mathews, Elezebeth, 109
Mathikettan Mala, 139–40
Matriliny, 37, 92
mechanised trawlers, 46
Medical College Vellore, 38
medicine, 38, 69, 77, 94, 128
Meher, Surendra, 94
Mencher, Joan P., 46–47

Menon, Akhil, 102
Menon, Dilip M., 33
Menon, P. N. C., 79
Menon, Vineetha
merchants, 10, 17, 24–27, 33–34,
    68, 91
Mfar, 72
Michael Tharakan, P. K., 26–27, 35
migrant, 11, 12, 27, 39, 48–50, 73,
    78–79, 82–93, 96–98, 106, 114–15,
    126–27, 129, 146, 148
migration, 8–13, 16–17, 24–27, 33,
    38, 43, 47, 49, 54, 62, 64–65,
    73, 82–98, 103, 106, 109, 112,
    114, 117–18, 132, 139–40, 141,
    145–46
    capitalism, 95–96
    consumption–saving connection,
        87–89
    immigration, 96–98
    skill connection, 89–90
    women who moved, 92–95
    women who stayed back, 91–92
mining, 51, 135, 140
Mishra, Udaya Shankar, 96
missionaries, 11, 31, 34, 38, 102
missions, 6, 11, 22, 31–35, 37–38, 40,
    88, 102, 115–16, 125, 128, 131,
    136–37, 149
Mohamed Ali, P., 72
Mohanan Pillai, P., 59–61
Mohanty, S. K., 87
moneylending, 29
monsoon, 10, 41, 43–44, 134, 141
Mukherjee, Robin, 8
Mullaperiyar dam, 136
Muslims, 17, 21–22, 37, 85, 115, 117,
    119–20, 127
Muthoot Finance, 74, 77–78
Muwonge, Abdu, 113
Mysore, 17–20

Nair, Sreelekha, 85, 94
Namboodiripad, E. M. S., 121
Nambudris, 20
Narasimhan, B., 142
Narayana, D., 97
National and Quilon Bank, 29
National Family Health Survey, 104
National Sample Survey, 115–16, 125
Nayars, 20–22, 32
Neethi, P., 34, 102
Nelliyambathi, 140
Nepal, 84
Nesamony, Sam, 38
neutraceuticals, 77, 79–80
Nipah virus outbreak, 55
North America, 12, 70, 146
nurses, 38–39, 85, 93–95
nursing, 11, 38–39, 91, 93–94, 103–04, 129

Ockhi cyclone, 55
Oommen, Ginu Zacharia, 87
Oommen, M. A., 29, 61, 113
Osella, Caroline, 95
Osella, Filippo, 95
Oterra, 71

paddy, 23–24, 31, 41–48, 51–52, 129–30, 138–39
Padmanabhan, M., 59, 138
Padmanabhan, Nirmala, 59
Pakistan, 84
panchayats, 113, 128, 130–32
Panikar, P. G. K., 44, 104–05, 107
Parambikulam wildlife sanctuary, 140
Parida, Jajati K., 87, 90, 97
Parida, J. K., 90, 97
Patnaik, Prabhat, 3–4
Pattadath, Bindhulakshmi, 94
Peirce Leslie, 28
pepper, 18–19, 23–25, 53, 64, 80, 101

per capita income, 1, 5, 7, 109, 110
Persia, 17
Persian Gulf migration, 8–9, 11, 67, 79, 82–87, 98. See also Gulf
Perumbavoor, 73, 96
Peter, Benoy, 73, 96–97
Pillai, V. R., 44
Plachimada, 137
plantations, 9, 10, 12, 16, 24–28, 31, 36, 42, 45, 48, 50, 52–54, 56, 58, 60, 63–66, 71–72, 80–81, 101, 121–23, 125–26, 135–36, 138–39, 142
Plant Lipids, 71
plywood, 70, 73, 78, 96, 146
pollution, 39, 135–37
Ponnani, 17–18
population density, 41, 44, 106, 140
Portuguese, 16–17, 33
Prasad, G., 138
Praveen, Anandu, 87
princely states, 6, 9, 12, 19, 26, 30, 36, 39, 41, 53, 61–62, 66, 69–70, 83, 100–01, 103, 105, 145
public distribution, 55, 129–30, 147
public finance, 113–14
public health, 38, 105–06, 108, 128–29
Purayil, Mufsin Puthan, 85
Pushpangadan, P., 47

Qadeer, Imrana, 105

Radhakrishnan, P., 122
railways, 24, 26
rainfall, 14, 55, 134–35, 142, 145
Ramanathan, Mala, 96
Ramaswamy Iyer, C. P., 30, 136
Rama Varma III, 20
Rama Varma V, 32–33
Ramesh, M. V., 138
Ram Mohan, K. T. (Rammohan, K. T.), 4, 30, 62, 122

Ravindranathan Nair, K., 70
Ravi Pillai, B., 79
Ravi Raman, K., 4, 12, 14, 28, 62, 87,
    90, 97, 120, 122, 124, 126, 136–37,
    140, 142
Reddy, Sujani K., 38, 93
religion, 17, 22, 37, 39
remittances, 9, 12, 43, 47, 49–50, 58,
    62–63, 66–67, 77, 83, 85–91,
    95–96, 111–12, 114–15, 125, 129,
    132–33, 143, 145–46
rice, 10, 23, 26, 41, 44–45, 55, 129–30,
    138–39
Roy, Tirthankar, 19, 86
rubber, 12, 23–25, 28–29, 52–53, 57,
    61, 63–65, 69–70, 72–73, 78, 81,
    134–35, 146
Rubfila, 72

Sajitha, A., 64
Sami-Sabinsa, 79–80
Sanjeev Nair, 77
Sarkar, Subrata, 8
Scheduled Caste, 115–17, 125
Scheduled Tribe, 115, 117, 124–25
Sen, Amartya, 7, 99
Shibulal, S. D., 76
Siegmann, Karin Astrid, 85
Silent Valley, 136
Silicon Valley, 75
Singh, Anjana, 19
slavery, 26, 30–31
Slavery Abolition Act, 211
social justice, 3, 108
soil erosion, 14, 55, 135
Soman, C. R., 105
spices, 10, 12, 17–18, 23–24, 28, 39–40,
    52–53, 56, 62–65, 67, 69–74, 78,
    81, 134, 146
Spices Board, 64
Sreerupa, 89

Sri Lanka, 84–85
state capacity, 36, 39, 101, 113, 146
Sterling Farm Research, 72
Stokes, Eric, 2
Subhiksha Keralam, 55
Subrahmanian, K. K., 61
Sudheer, K. P., 142
Sujathan, P. K., 90
Sukumaran Nair, M. K., 49–50
Sultan, Tipu, 18, 20
Sunny, Justin, 97
Synthite, 71
Syrian Christians, 26–27, 29, 33, 37,
    39–40, 63–64

Tamil Nadu, 1, 7, 42, 46, 58, 61, 63, 66,
    72, 96, 109, 129, 144
tapioca, 14, 23, 41, 55
Tata Finlay, 60
tea, 10, 23–28, 31–32, 52–53, 56, 58,
    60–65, 72, 78, 80, 134–35
technology, 12, 43, 47, 55, 59, 66–67,
    69–70, 75, 78, 80–81, 103, 113, 131,
    136, 142, 146
Technopark, 75–76
Telangana, 1, 7
Tellicherry (Thalassery), 17–18
tenancy, 21–22, 33, 48–49, 122–24
Thakur, Manish, 85
Thalassery (Tellicherry), 17–18
Thampy, M. M., 61
Tharian George, K., 28, 65
Thieme, Susan, 85
Thiruvananthapuram Medical College,
    128
Thomas, Alfred Vedam, 72
Thomas Isaac, T. M., 26, 58
Thomas, J., 142
Thomas, Jayan Jose, 8, 61
Thomas, K. T., 25–26
Thomas, Neethu, 95

Thomas, Susan, 21, 32
Thrissur, 70, 72–74, 79, 137–38
timber, 10, 17, 23–24, 26, 28, 39–40,
    63, 73–74
Timmons, Stephen, 94
Tiruvitamkur, 30
T. K. M., 76
tourism, 12, 67–71, 76, 79, 81, 112, 134,
    139, 143, 147–49
trade (trading), 10–11, 16–20, 23–31,
    40–43, 45–50, 52–54, 56–66,
    69–71, 73–74, 76–79, 81–82, 84,
    86, 111–12, 114, 119, 134, 147–49
trade unions, 42, 45–48, 50, 54, 58–61
trading firms, 23, 25, 28, 30, 38, 58–59,
    63–64, 69, 74
Travancore, 6, 10, 16–40, 56–57, 59,
    63–64, 69, 81, 100–01, 104–05, 121,
    127–28, 130, 135–36, 144–45
tree crops, 23, 27–28, 36, 39–41, 51–54,
    57, 101

unemployment, 3, 14, 42–43, 48, 49,
    82, 84–85, 102, 148–49
United Nations, 3, 55
urbanization, 90, 125, 138–41, 143

Vajra, 72
Vakkom Mohammed Abdul Khader
    Moulavi, 25
Valatheeswaran, C., 88
Varelaz, Maria Villares, 98
Varier, P. S., 69
Varma, Divya, 97
Varma, Martanda, 18, 20, 25, 32–33

Vasco Da Gama, 17
Vema, V. K., 142
Vembanad Lake, 44, 137, 139
Venkiteswaran, C. S., 97
Venture capital, 76
Vijaylaxmi Cashews, 70–71

wages, 21, 25, 30–33, 40, 42–44, 46–51,
    53–54, 57–59, 61, 63–66, 74, 85,
    94, 96–98, 126, 146
Wallace, Sally, 113
Wayanad, 24–25, 27–28, 137–38
West Asia, 10, 16, 70, 134
West Bengal, 13, 45, 56, 73–74, 96,
    119–20, 144, 148
William Goodacre, 28
women, 32, 34, 37–39, 54, 57–58,
    63, 68, 75, 80, 82, 83, 85, 88,
    91–95, 100–02, 104, 106, 108,
    113–17, 128, 131, 147–48. See also
    migration
Women and Children Hospital, 128
workers, 2, 11, 13, 21, 24–25, 28, 31–34,
    42, 44, 46, 48–51, 54, 58, 60, 62,
    73–75, 78, 84–85, 90, 94, 96–98,
    102, 121–23, 125–27, 130, 136, 146,
    148. See also labour
World Trade Organization (WTO), 53
World War I, 31
World War II, 64–65, 70, 130

Yusuff Ali, M. A., 75, 79

Zachariah, K. C., 86, 89–90, 108
zamorin, 18–19

Printed in the United States
by Baker & Taylor Publisher Services